CAROL SHIELDS AND THE

Throughout her literary and critical career, Canadian writer Carol Shields (1935–2003) resisted simple categorization. Her novels are elegant puzzles that confront the reader with the ambiguity of meaning and narrative, yet their position within Shields' critical feminist project has, until now, been obscured.

In *Carol Shields and the Writer-Critic*, Brenda Beckman-Long illuminates that project through the study of Shields' extensive oeuvre, including her fiction and criticism. Beckman-Long brings depth to her analysis through close readings of six novels, including the award-winning *The Stone Diaries*. Elliptical, open-ended, and concerned with women writing about women, these novels reveal Shields' critique of dominant masculine discourses and her deep engagement with the long tradition of women's life writing. Beckman-Long's original archival research attests to Shields' preoccupation with the changing efforts of waves of feminist activism and writing.

A much needed reappraisal of Shields' innovative work, *Carol Shields and the Writer-Critic* contributes to the scholarship on life writing and autobiography, literary criticism, and feminist and critical theory.

BRENDA BECKMAN-LONG is an assistant professor of English at Briercrest College and Seminary, which is affiliated with the University of Saskatchewan.

Carol Shields and the Writer-Critic

BRENDA BECKMAN-LONG

UNIVERSITY OF TORONTO PRESS
Toronto Buffalo London

© University of Toronto Press 2015
Toronto Buffalo London
www.utppublishing.com

ISBN 978-1-4426-4570-7 (cloth)   ISBN 978-1-4426-1395-9 (paper)

Library and Archives Canada Cataloguing in Publication

Beckmen-Long, Brenda, author
Carol Shields and the writer-critic / Brenda Beckman-Long.

Includes bibliographical references and index.
ISBN 978-1-4426-4570-7 (bound)   ISBN 978-1-4426-1395-9 (paperback)

1. Shields, Carol, 1935–2003 – Criticism and interpretation.   2. Women
and literature.   3. Feminist literary criticism   I. Title.

PS8587.H46Z6 2015   C813'.54   C2015-905935-6

This book has been published with the generous assistance of Briercrest
College and Seminary.

University of Toronto Press acknowledges the financial assistance to its
publishing program of the Canada Council for the Arts and the Ontario
Arts Council, an agency of the Government of Ontario.

Canada Council
for the Arts

Conseil des Arts
du Canada

ONTARIO ARTS COUNCIL
CONSEIL DES ARTS DE L'ONTARIO
an Ontario government agency
un organisme du gouvernement de l'Ontario

Funded by the
Government
of Canada

Financé par le
gouvernement
du Canada

Canadä

For my mother and grandmother, Isabelle Albert Beckman and Mary Meszaros Albert

Contents

Acknowledgements

During the research and writing of this book, I received assistance from the Social Sciences and Humanities Research Council of Canada in the form of a Post-doctoral Fellowship at McMaster University as well as a Canada Graduate Scholarship Doctoral Award. I also received a PhD Scholarship and a research grant from the University of Alberta and Briercrest College and Seminary, respectively, in addition to travel grants from the Association of Canadian College and University Teachers of English.

I am particularly grateful and indebted to Christine Wiesenthal for her insightful suggestions and readings of my drafts as well as her gracious support throughout this project. I thank her, Daniel Coleman, and the anonymous readers for their many helpful comments on the manuscript. I also thank my editors, Siobhan McMenemy, Kel Pero, and Frances Mundy, for their support and fine editorial assistance. For thoughtful comments at other stages of the research and writing, I acknowledge Susanna Egan, Jo-Ann Wallace, Cecily Devereux, Lynn Penrod, Nora Stovel, Heather Zwicker, Timothy Long, Joanne Muzak, and Kate Baltais.

I wish to acknowledge, too, Catherine Hobbs and Lynne Lafontaine who assisted me with the Carol Shields Fonds at the Library and Archives Canada, and Don Shields who gave me permission to use the papers in the Shields archive. I am equally grateful to the editors, John C. Ball and Jennifer Andrews, at *Studies in Canadian Literature* for permission to reprint sections of my article on *The Stone Diaries*; the fourth chapter here was previously published in a different form under the title of "*The Stone Diaries* as an 'Apocryphal Journal'" in their scholarly journal.

My gratitude also extends to the members of Lit Group, including Kathy Berriman, Daniel and Wendy Coleman, Gary Diver, Leila and Shawn Dueck, Allison Fizzard, Francesco Freddolini, Tara Gish, Brian Herman, Grace Kehler, Jeff La Rocque, Michelle Lipka, Russell Mang, Yvonne Petry, Scott Pittendrigh, Annalisa Raho, and Jerry and Patti Sherk for their encouragement, friendship, and passion for literature over the years. My further thanks go to Lorne Kish and Liz Borgel, Cameron Kish, and Violet Kish for welcoming me into their homes on my research trips.

My heartfelt gratitude goes out, finally, to my mother, Isabelle Albert Beckman, for sharing with me her love of reading and languages, and to my husband, Timothy Long, for offering me his constant companionship and enduring belief in me and my writing.

Permissions

Cover art by Mary Pratt, *Christmas Fire*, 1981, oil on masonite, 76.2 × 59.7 cm. Used with permission of the artist and the Musée d'art contemporain de Montréal, Lavalin Collection.

From Margaret Atwood's poem "Another Night Visit," published in *Tributaries: An Anthology: Writer to Writer*, edited by Barry Dempster (Oakville: Mosaic Press, 1978, p. 60). Collection copyright © Barry Dempster, 1978. Used with permission of the author.

From Pat Lowther's "Woman On/Against Snow," published in *Milk Stone* (Ottawa: Borealis, 1974, pp. 15–16). Used with permission of Borealis Press.

From Pat Lowther's "Kitchen Murder," "City Slide / 6," and "Last Letter to Pablo," published in *The Collected Works of Pat Lowther* (Edmonton: NeWest Press, 2010, pp. 237, 234, 221, respectively), edited by Christine Wiesenthal. Used with permission of NeWest Press.

From Seymour Mayne's poem "For Pat Lowther (1935–1975)," published in *The Impossible Promised Land: Poems New and Selected* (Oakville: Mosaic Press, 1981, p. 118). Used with permission of the author.

From Daniel David Moses's poem "Our Lady of the Glacier," published in *First Person Plural* (Windsor: Black Moss Press, 1988, pp. 46–7), edited by Judith Fitzgerald. Used with permission of the author and Black Moss Press.

From P.K. Page's poem in "Pat Lowther: A Tribute," published in *Contemporary Verse Two* 2.1 (1976): 15–17. Used with permission of the Estate of P.K. Page.

From Elizabeth Brewster's poem in "Pat Lowther: A Tribute,"
   published in *Contemporary Verse Two* 2.1 (1976): 15–17. Reprinted
   in *Selected Poems of Elizabeth Brewster* (Ottawa: Oberon Press,
   1985). Used with permission of Oberon Press.
From *Carol Shields Fonds* in the Literary Collection of Library and
   Archives Canada. Used with permission of the Estate of Carol
   Shields.
Chapter 4 was published in a different form under the title of "*The
   Stone Diaries* as an 'Apocryphal Journal'" in *Studies in Canadian
   Literature* 35.1 (2010): 127–46.

CAROL SHIELDS AND THE WRITER-CRITIC

Shields as Writer-Critic: Autobiography and the Politics of Self-Representation

Canadian novelist Carol Shields was the first writer ever to win both the Pulitzer Prize and the Governor General's Award for Fiction. In the same year that she published *The Stone Diaries* (1993), the novel that attracted these awards, she also published an essay entitled "Arriving Late: Starting Over." In this essay she tells of a provocative discovery about contemporary critical theory: "Literary theory was not, after all, the motor that drove writing forward; theory was no more than an eager young fresh-faced yardworker, intent on raking up the leaves as they fell from the tree, trying to make sense of them, hoping to arrange them in comprehensible piles" (247). As a writer and critic who published her first novel at the age of forty, Shields adds, "I was rather late in discovering this fact. We need serious critical analysis, of course, but not the throttling sort of theorizing that proclaims and forbids and ultimately places limits on fiction's possibilities." Shields's essay is a personal and critical manifesto. In all of her writing Shields initiates what she calls "an inquiry into language" ("Arriving" 251), particularly the possibilities of women's writing in their critical, literary, and autobiographical works. Most importantly, she investigates the potential for fiction to offer a feminist critique of dominant discourses such as autobiography and critical theory. Her short fiction is designed to be a "story-as-container," an envelope or fold of language ("Arriving" 249, 251). Her novels likewise contain "a fiction that form[s] a sort of pocket for its own exegesis" (246). Her intent clearly emerges in *Swann* (1987), which was nominated for the Governor General's Award, and for which she worked out a structure of embedded narratives, only after setting aside that novel to create the narrative "pockets" of the short stories in *Various Miracles*

(1985). Shields uses enfolding and embedding techniques again in *The Republic of Love* (1992) and *The Stone Diaries* (1993). In her final novel, *Unless* (2002), the structural metaphor of a fold signifies a narrative return and ethical response to the critical challenges of post-modernism and post-colonialism to feminist theory. Throughout her work, Shields experiments to blend metafiction with life writing in order to explore critically women's practices of self-representation. By considering the trajectory of her body of work, we discover that Carol Shields's political project extends from feminist critique to cultural critique; in gathering the leaves of her oeuvre, we can find traces of important cultural shifts from critical theory to political and ethical practices.

The Stone Diaries provides a ready model of the metafictional structure that Shields designs for critical purposes. The novel reads at the outset as a fictional autobiography of Daisy Goodwill, an ordinary woman whose life is traced from her birth in Stonewall, Manitoba, to her death in a Florida retirement home. But her life story ends with an odd statement: "'I am not at peace.' / Daisy Goodwill's final (unspoken) words" (361). While the declaration appears in the first person, it is quoted by an unnamed narrator. Daisy's voice is either ghostly or imagined, unsettling the account of Daisy's life of eighty years. It raises many questions. Who is authorized to write an autobiography? Whose life is regarded as significant enough to make history? Reading backwards, we find that the statement recalls the unidentified narrator, who, midway through the novel, characterizes the text as an "apocryphal journal" (118). Is this an unauthorized and alternative history? What are the implications of an apocryphal history – one that is perhaps narrated by a daughter or granddaughter, as suggested by the novel's opening poem, which is entitled "The Grandmother Cycle." Even the novel's title suggests not a diary but several diaries. In addition to the generic ambiguity, textual clues indicate a life story that is embedded in a family narrative compiled from many sources. They include Daisy's diaries, letters, and columns, as well as the diaries of her father and husband. Upon further reflection, we see that the life story resists the categories of autobiography and biography. Along with the text's subversion of gender stereotypes, including daughter, mother, and crone, it explores the injustice of suppressing women's voices and their stories. These social and ethical contexts lend meaning and resonance to Daisy's final unsettling words. In the retold and unauthorized version of her life, readers encounter shifting figures of the woman writer in not only Daisy but also her daughters.

The novel is Shields's preferred form for her discursive and political practice, in part because of its multi-voicedness and hybridity, and in part because of its history as "the only form in which women [have] participated fully, from the beginning" (Shields, *Austen* 26). The novel's narrative voice and characters create a polyphony that engages with the language of others. Shields also observes in her literary criticism that women writers in Canada – ranging from Frances Brooke and Susanna Moodie to Margaret Laurence and Alice Munro – cross generic boundaries to embed autobiography in fiction ("My Craft" 150–1, "Three" 54). By strategically positioning herself as part of national and international traditions of women's life writing, which are historical and ongoing and which have the capacity to interrogate "the established tradition" ("Thinking" 12–13), Shields resists the postmodern notion of "the death of the novel" (Shields, qtd. in Denoon 11). She shows that the novel is alive on the frontier of experimentation and the frontier has moved "womanward" (Shields, qtd. in Hollenberg 353). For Shields the writing process remains open-ended, contingent, and dynamic, as her enfolding, elliptical, and spiralling narratives demonstrate by embracing "both contradiction and tentativeness" ("Arriving" 248–9). Because it is so open-ended and enigmatic, the narrative spiral offers, in effect, a textual resistance to both transparency and critical interpretation. Shields's ambiguous texts are cleverly designed to expose the act of reading itself as a political project. Readers become engaged in a search for meaning and a struggle to control it, finding themselves in a trap or narrative game; at the same time, the author becomes a writer-critic. With this type of complexity – and, at the same time, economy of style and apparent accessibility – Shields's texts are like elegant puzzles.

Shields's novels and political project recall Quebec novelist Nicole Brossard's idea of the writer-critic as a strategic stance for women: "les femmes syncrones, celles-ci étant l'écrivaine et la critique" ("Mouvements" 229).[1] Brossard envisions women's writing, even novels, as critical texts. She calls for texts that are elliptical and spiralling, employing the narrative strategies of irony, parody, intertextuality, and embedded myths and stories, especially women's stories. Narratologist Wallace Martin further argues that "when a writer talks about a narrative within that narrative," by means of parody and metafiction, "the writer has become a theorist"; these strategies signal more than "game-playing," because at stake is "the whole system of traditional distinctions between reality and fiction on the one hand and truth and falsity on the other" (181). Such strategies can in the long term challenge political or social realities. Just as Shields does, Brossard calls for an ethical criticism that poses questions and enacts struggles, particularly intellectual quests for language to embody that for which one would otherwise lack words. This type of women's writing, or "écriture féminine" (228), possesses the ambiguity and complexity necessary to make space for desire and thought, pleasure and reflection, writer and reader. In short, it creates an interactive space. In these ways, she thinks that women's bodies and bodies of writing can activate and illuminate new understandings, a position shared by Shields. A West Coast contemporary and novelist, Daphne Marlatt, coins the term "fictionalysis" for a similar vision of women's writing ("Self-Representation" 202). The body of Shields's writing certainly exhibits the narrative strategies of irony, parody, self-reflexivity, and *mises en abyme* that recur in her novels and that constitute an inquiry into language, including the language of criticism. In a supposedly post-feminist age, Shields charts the way for new forms of women's activism.

Much like Shields, Marlatt views narrative as a labyrinth of language – that is, "a continuous walking that folds back on itself and in folding back moves forward" ("Writing" 45). Such movement is possible because "women know the slippery feel of language, the walls that exclude us, the secret passageways of double meaning ... the meaning our negated (in language) bodies radiate." The writing body, like the body of writing, suggests multiple meanings. The narrative space is a mirroring maze, a web of interconnecting passages that relates "what the writer meant to what the reader understands, in a commune-ication" (45–6). It is the communicative function of the text as a social practice that invites a close examination in Shields's work. Her novels intentionally contain "the lives of women whose stories [have] more to do with the texture of ordinary life and the spirit of community than with personal battles, goals, and prizes" in a masculine-dominated literary tradition ("Arriving" 249). In fact, if her narratives find any resolution at all, it may be, paradoxically, in the silences and gaps that suggest alternative courses of action in the language of the other. Shields insists that her short stories turn "on some variable of language, the failure of language ... its gaps and silences" in order to put a "torque on ordinary discourse" (250). This strategy is evident in not only her short stories but also her novels, especially in their embedded and autobiographical self-representations.

Larry Weller, the main character in *Larry's Party*, is a maker of labyrinths or mazes, like the novelist herself who constructs life narratives mainly for female characters by transforming the labyrinthine space of autobiography. Speaking of his art, Larry stresses that mazes "make perfect sense only when you look down on them from above" (219). He adds, "A maze is designed so that we get to be part of the art." Similarly, Shields uses self-representation in increasingly complex ways over the course of her career, as she embeds autobiographical discourses in metafiction. Embedded narratives or mises en abyme transform the novel into a commentary on writing and contemporary criticism. The later novels, in particular, position readers with a distanced view of a writer's life story.

Most of Shields's main characters are women writers. Judith Gill in *Small Ceremonies* and Charleen Forrest in *The Box Garden* are a biographer and a poet, respectively, and their journals unfold as gendered confessions. These journals span a period of crisis and resist autobiography especially when read together as not the work of an autonomous self, but the interaction of two sisters. In *Swann*, the life of poet Mary Swann is embedded in the stories of her critics whose multiple voices form a fragmented narrative. Biographical resemblances between the fictional Swann and Canadian poet Pat Lowther further challenge readers' assumptions about the boundaries between fiction and non-fiction, especially their ideological effects. The embedded narratives create a heightened perception of intersubjectivity and call for an ethical criticism by laying bare social hierarchies and categories. *The Republic of Love* is a metafiction that alternates between the lives of writer and critic Fay McLeod and broadcaster Tom Avery until their stories are interwoven. In *The Stone Diaries*, diarist and columnist Daisy Goodwill disappears in the narrative maze of her own story's telling, unless it is read as embedded in a family narrative and retelling by her granddaughter and daughter. This narrative functions as an apocryphal history, and meta-autobiography, to interrogate both autobiography and historiography. Finally, *Unless* returns to confessional and autobiographical strategies to record a crisis in the life of novelist Reta Winters.

With surprisingly ironic twists this meta-autobiography questions the ethics of the feminist subject.

These novels display the double strategies and embeddedness of autobiographical and fictional discourses, signalling Shields's dual interests in language and the politics of self-representation. Her narratives map the limits of both in complex, sophisticated, and self-reflexive texts. Shields herself describes the mise en abyme in *The Stone Diaries*: "There's a sort of postmodern box-within-the-box, within-the-box. I mean, I'm writing the novel, and I'm writing her life, and I'm writing her knowledge of her life" (Shields, qtd. in Joan Thomas 58). In *Unless*, she depicts again the novelist writing about a novelist who is writing. Shields is interested in "the idea of trying to catch a life in some way" (Shields, qtd. in Maharaj 11). Because of an equal interest in the politics of telling, her self-reflexivity and irony distance readers from the main character. Shields employs other postmodern strategies, such as fragmented narratives and mixed genres, to challenge not only male authority (Shields, qtd. in Anderson 147) but also critical authority. As she states in an interview with Eleanor Wachtel, "Some postmodernists think there is no point beyond the language game, but I think there can be" ("Interview" 44). Her double strategies and complex frames, including the metafictional structure of the mise en abyme and the genre of autobiography, deliberately focus attention on the self and others, creating textual ambiguities and productive tensions. Such tensions complicate and denaturalize our assumptions about relationships between the individual and society or fiction and non-fiction. In Shields's work, the novels' elliptical and enigmatic textual action, as well as their content, reproduce and expose the complex interactions of art and life, writer and critic, writer and reader.

The distancing effect of the mise en abyme becomes evident when one thinks of the novel in terms of the narrative communication situation: a chain of dialogue from the implied author to the narrator and then to the implied reader. The narrator is distanced from the main character in novels that are narrated in the third person. Even in the first person of fictional autobiographies and confessional novels, the narrating-I is distanced from the narrated-I. The implied author and implied reader are, moreover, distanced from the main character or ideological subject. Distance is also achieved by the use of irony. An ironic tone must be attributed not only to the narrator, but to the implied author. At the same time, the implied author cannot be identified with the real author who is unavailable in the text. Instead, the implied author must be seen as a fictional construct that is inferred and assembled by the reader from the text as a whole, including its complex irony and parody. In these ways, the main character becomes an object of inquiry even in the autobiographical narrative. The represented life becomes a model, and the narrative takes on the spectral quality of a hyperreal simulation, as it does in *The Stone Diaries*, *The Republic of Love*, and all the novels in question. As critical theorist Jean Baudrillard states, the real is produced from discursive matrices and the hyperreal is "the product of an irradiating synthesis of combinatory models in a hyperspace" (3). These terms equally apply to the life story of the main character and the text itself, which is a discursive hybrid of fictional and autobiographical discourses.

Through the frame of autobiography or life writing Shields draws readers' attention not only to the represented life but also to the genre. In relation to the maze of a life narrative, the reader occupies a godlike subject position by looking down from above, and, in some cases, the represented life is allegorical even as it appears in the cautionary tale of *Swann* or the *memento mori* of *The Stone Diaries*. But Shields's novels offer more than the postmodern irony suggested by this reading. In recent autobiographical practices among women, Leigh Gilmore observes, the genre is a simulation of real life; she characterizes the autobiographical space as both an "engendering matrix of textual selfhood" and a labyrinth of history and language that women writers must negotiate (*Autobiographics* 63–5). Shields's novels are characterized by not only an ironic twist, but also a feminist twist in a complex cultural critique. Viewed politically, her works valorize women's narratives, just as other life writing is designed to do (Kadar, *Essays* 10). In the guise of a game, her novels reposition the reader and critic in relation to the represented lives. Shields's texts simultaneously produce postmodernist and feminist readings of these lives, leaving readers to judge or identify with the woman writer, depending upon their own critical or political commitments. In this way, each text "reads" as well as divides its critics. Shields uses feminist theory to break with critical theory, a practice sustained throughout her career.

Shields's novels demonstrate this double strategy in her use of tone. Although the novels are ironic, the woman writer is depicted in a crisis so that the tone is also politically urgent, at least implicitly.

The political aspect of her work evolved over the years. Looking back, Shields notes, "I was writing feminist stories [previously] that didn't look like feminist stories. I had an agenda, but I didn't make it very clear." With *Unless*, the urgency becomes explicit. About second-wave feminism Shields argues, "It was the biggest move-ment of the century. A lot of people think the playing field has been levelled, but I don't agree" (Shields, qtd. in Aikins 69). An earlier novel, *The Stone Diaries*, has an implicitly tragic tone, for "any woman in this century can understand what it feels like to be erased from the culture" (Shields, qtd. in Joan Thomas 60). But in the context of third-wave feminisms in the late twentieth and early twenty-first centuries – theory that has absorbed the poststructuralist and post-colonial challenges to universal categories such as *woman* – Shields's works produce not only ironic, but also political effects. While such narrative strategies appear to varying degrees in all of her novels, including those with male protagonists (*Larry's Party* and *Happen-stance*), my study focuses on the novels that depict women writers. In these novels, which include *Small Ceremonies*, *The Box Garden*, *Swann*, *The Republic of Love*, *The Stone Diaries*, and *Unless*, Shields's "woman-ward" project is most clearly evident. This study also provides a new reading of Shields's critical contribution to a historical tradition of women's life writing in terms of autobiographical strategies, while reinterpreting Shield's novels as a body of work that represents a significant and sustained political project.

The fiction of Carol Shields has been compared at times to that of Margaret Laurence, a Canadian writer of a previous generation who shared a critical vision of making women's voices heard. Just as Lau-rence's body of work has undergone a reappraisal since the 1980s, so too, the time has come for a reassessment of Shields's oeuvre. Critic George Woodcock recognizes Laurence as "the best living Canadian novelist" in 1980 (157), but in 2000 he calls Shields "a popular novel-ist ... pursuing a line of comfortable Canadian realism" (qtd. in "The 90s" 41). But Shields is, like Laurence, more than a popular novel-ist. Woodcock assumes that Shields merely reproduces a realism that Laurence helped to establish, rather than attending to the feminist project with which her work engages. Shields seeks even to extend it. Woodcock's criticism ignores Shields's stated ambivalence towards the "brick house" of prairie realism and fails to take into account her embrace of parody and pastiche. Demonstrating a more nuanced view than Woodcock, Shields admires Laurence's use of fictional autobiography and uses many of the same strategies as Laurence, including experiments with double-voicedness in gendered confessions and the mise en abyme of the writer-as-character in *The Diviners*. Shields's interest lies in transforming women's life stories and the autobiographical possibilities of "the arc of a whole life when it curves" (Shields, qtd. in Maharaj 11). By doing so she advances the feminist movement in Canada to address the next generation.

Instead of being situated in a tradition of Canadian realism, as Woodcock proposes, Shields is best placed in a growing tradition of women's life writing in Canada since the 1970s, and an even broader tradition of international autobiography studies identified by feminist theorists such as Leigh Gilmore, Sidonie Smith, and Susanna Egan. While some critics have read individual works by Shields through the lenses of autobiography studies and women's life writing, a comprehensive reassessment of her oeuvre from these theoretical perspectives is needed. Woodcock admits that Shields's craftsmanship aims at something more, but he and others fail to identify the wide scope of her political project. It is evident from this oversight that Shields positions herself almost too successfully as part of a women's writing tradition that resists literary and critical categories.

Since the turn of the millennium Susanna Egan and Gabriele Helms have observed a lack of attention to the genres and poetics of autobiography despite a proliferation of autobiographical practices in Canada (6). They point out that "the time has surely come to combine generic and theoretical considerations quite specifically with Canadian texts" (9). Interestingly, Shirley Neuman and Helen Buss made the same observation more than a decade earlier. These critics have laid the groundwork for a new understanding and recontextualization of Shields's work.

Like her contemporaries, Shields exposes political targets that are aligned with what Gilmore calls a masculine tradition of autobiography and its realisms (*Autobiographics* 1, 65). Accordingly, Shields's fiction plays with the characteristics of the postmodern novel, such as non-linearity, the decentred subject, irony, parody, self-reflexivity, mixed genres, historical grounding, and critique (Hutcheon, "Power" 41; "Postmodernism" 612). The later novels in particular are theoretically and politically informed with a feminist standpoint that is postmodern and materialist. These novels model the type of feminist critique that is described by Rosemary Hennessy, who, as another contemporary of Shields, sees the real as a discursive and material force (126). She values women's autobiography for reinterpreting the real, since women's lives (and men's) are shaped by ideology and never beyond the reach of theory. Similar to Shields, Hennessy calls for a feminist critique that "*begins with* inquiry into and opposition to the devaluation of 'woman' under patriarchy in all of the relations of production it spans" (97, original emphasis). These include not only individual and domestic relations, but also collective and economic ones, such as relations with publishers, editors, and critics, which are addressed in Shields's portrayals of women writers. A feminist critique is aligned with other discourses including poststructuralism when it presents a discursive subject that challenges notions of autonomy and essentialism. Even so, a feminist critique involves a double-voicedness, such as the double twist of tone in Shields's novels. Parody itself offers a double encoding – that is, "two codes" with "one message" (Martin 179–80). Accordingly, Shields's parody presents a unified message that is political in the form of a feminist critique. Also implicit in her work is a broader cultural critique, for she never treats language or representation as a transparent vehicle of knowledge despite her focus on the lives of ordinary women. With increasing sophistication over the course of her career, Shields's novels reinscribe a consistent, complex, feminist critique of a masculine-dominated literary history and criticism.

Shields traces her feminist awakening to her reading of Betty Friedan during the Women's Movement in the 1960s and graduate studies with feminist Lorraine McMullen at the University of Ottawa in the 1970s (Shields, qtd. in Wachtel, "Interview" 26). She self-consciously positions herself as part of a literary tradition of women's writing, ranging from English novelists such as Jane Austen, Virginia Woolf, and Margaret Drabble, to Canadian writers such as Gabrielle Roy, Margaret Laurence, Margaret Atwood, and Alice Munro, all of whom take women's lives as their explicit subjects. She claims a special affinity to Austen who "demonstrates how large narratives can occupy small spaces" (Shields, qtd. in Hollenberg 346). Like Laurence's novels, Shields's works can be characterized as fictional autobiographies even though her later novels, especially *Swann*, *The Stone Diaries*, and *Unless*, are often considered more experimental and postmodern than her earlier ones, such as *Small Ceremonies*, *The Box Garden*, and *The Republic of Love*.[2] For this reason, the later works draw more critical attention, while the earlier works are relatively neglected, though recent collections of essays do begin to address the early fiction and works in other genres. Unlike Laurence, however, Shields's works are more ironic than tragic, with a parodic edge that is Austen-like and rapier-sharp.

Shields's use of autobiographical space and self-representational discourses to reinscribe a feminist critique offers a compelling subject from the perspective of international autobiography studies. By the late 1980s and 1990s, when Shields wrote her best-known works, feminist theorists were expanding the critical practices and poetics of women's autobiography. Evolving alongside feminist criticisms of the period, Shields's work embodies many of the issues articulated by critics, such as Smith, Gilmore, and Egan. Sidonie Smith recalls Philippe Lejeune's characterization of autobiography as a social contract to discuss its status as a cultural construct and artifice.[3] She also uses Mikhail Bakhtin's concept of dialogism to contest an essential and unified self. Like Shields, Smith thinks of the self as a multiple construct located in diverse and intersecting discourses (48). She believes women autobiographers position themselves rhetorically "in relation to cultural ideologies and figures of selfhood," but from these figures women are doubly estranged. A woman writer may therefore produce a complex double-voicedness or polyphony, creating "a fragile heteroglossia of her own" (50). She defines autobiography loosely as "a historically situated practice of self-representation," and the autobiographical mode as "an intersubjective exchange," not of truth, but a shared understanding of a life (Smith and Watson 13–14). Her emphasis is epistemological rather than ontological, and Shields takes the same approach, as evidenced in *Swann*, *The Republic of Love*, and even the early novels.

Leigh Gilmore presents autobiography, similarly, not as a genre but rather as "discourses of self-representation" (*Autobiographics* 13). Precisely because autobiography can be understood as a discursive and social practice, the signature of the woman writer becomes the mark of her self-definition, a political agency that is performative ("Mark" 14):

> Autobiography provides a stage where women writers, born again in the act of writing, may experiment with reconstructing the various discourses – of representation, of ideology – in which their subjectivity has been formed ... The subject is already multiple, heterogeneous, even

conflicted, and these contradictions expose the technologies of autobiography. (*Autobiographics* 85)

Autobiographical writing is not static but dynamic, offering a "site
of resistance" (*Autobiographics* xv). Issues of authority and reception
come into play since autobiographers subvert dominant figures of
selfhood and, in the process, present a cultural critique. Gilmore
asserts that personal narratives give voice to historically silenced
and marginalized persons, who may penetrate "the labyrinths of
history and language to possess ... the engendering matrix of textual
selfhood" (*Autobiographics* 63). These ideas support Shields's understanding that autobiographical modes lend themselves to inquiry
and experimentation.

Susanna Egan expands the discussion of discursive subjects and
intersubjective perspectives that mark the period that Shields's writing engages. With the theorists already mentioned, Egan shares an
understanding of the autobiographical space as specular and artificial. She sees that dialogism and mixed genres characterize contemporary autobiography: "The mirror of my title [*Mirror Talk*] is
more constructive than reflective of the self. It foregrounds interaction between people, among genres, and between writers and
readers of autobiography" (12). She explains that an interactive
space is created by multiple-voiced structures that are often contes-
tatory, open-ended, and urgent. An emphasis on crisis – which is
particularly evident in *Unless* and Shields's earlier novels – shows
it to be decentring and potentially transformative. Writers use the
autobiographical space not to trace a linear self-development, but to
represent, spatially, simultaneously, and immediately, multiple perspectives and multiple identities (19). These issues are written large
in Shields's fiction, from the first novel to the last, and most notably
in *The Stone Diaries*.

Women writers such as Shields trouble the genre of autobiography
by blending it with the polyphony of the novel. Egan re-emphasizes
the use of irony and self-reflexivity. At the same time, she remarks
that not all texts are "dialogic in the same way or to the same degree.
What is curious, however, is to see varieties of dialogism at play in a
genre that has traditionally been very little given to irony or instability and rather prone to monologism" (Egan 23). These issues signal
a significant development in autobiographical practices, including
the meta-autobiography, a term that fits Shields's later works, *Unless*

and *The Stone Diaries*. While these practices are by no means exclusive to women's writing, they are especially evident in women's life writing. Egan reclaims for all autobiographers the feminist idea that the personal is political. Contemporary autobiography explores possibilities for change, while dramatizing lived experience as a realistic trope for resisting dominant representations of identity. The body is a component of identity and the grounds of experiential knowledge that is often explored for political purposes (Egan 4–5). Egan asserts that as a narrative strategy, the autobiographical mode is dynamic and rhetorically effective because its dialogism engages the reader in many voices, perspectives, identities, and interpretations: "Our experience of each text becomes part of its instability, part of its unresolved search for meaning" (228). Egan, Smith, and Gilmore are vital here for resituating Shields.

But by taking up the role of a writer-critic, Shields moves into new territory and approaches what might be called "ficto-criticism," a term coined by a fellow Canadian and art critic, Jeanne Randolph. From feminist and psychoanalytical perspectives, Randolph has mixed autobiography with criticism and encouraged collaborative writing among artists and critics in recent decades (242–3). In Canada, Australia, and elsewhere many writers take her lead to develop similar practices that are creative and critical. They cross genres and employ mises en abyme and reader-traps, much like Shields. By design ficto-criticism today is performative, engaging, political, and ethical.

In light of these developments in Canadian studies, autobiography studies, and feminist theories of autobiography, women's autobiographical writing can be interpreted as a form of resistance to ideologies of selfhood and individualism, especially the autonomous male self. Women writers such as Shields employ postmodernist strategies to challenge established genres and the unified self. These autobiographical and critical practices extend to fiction. Women often exploit the autobiographical space for rhetorical effects, including the appeal of the real and a cultural privileging of autobiography, for the purpose of inscribing a feminine subject and feminist critique. The rhetorical distance that can be achieved by irony and parody heightens the potential for a political critique, while creating a subject position that unsettles readers' expectations and ideological assumptions, and implicates readers in a cultural critique that is ongoing. It is in the context of an evolving feminist critique that the novels of Shields must be re-evaluated.[4]

By re-examining a representative body of work by Carol Shields, including *Small Ceremonies*, *The Box Garden*, *Swann*, *The Republic of Love*, *The Stone Diaries*, and *Unless*, we find that Shields offers an example par excellence of broader trends in literary and autobiographical practices of women writers, particularly narrative strategies for addressing gender ideologies, the problem of the subject, and the crisis of knowledge in the academy. These issues are raised by poststructuralist and feminist theorists alike in a cultural shift from critical theory to political practices. Feminist theory has also struggled with the category of *woman* and the experiential basis of authority for knowledge about women's lives. For instance, Hennessy has expanded the category of *woman*, rearticulated the subject of feminism as an object of inquiry, redefined a feminist standpoint and collective subject, and reclaimed the emancipatory aims of a feminist critique. Shields's own inquiry into these issues is conducted over the course of an entire literary career, culminating in the political urgency of her last novel, *Unless*. In her work we can trace a cultural shift from second-wave feminism, especially in terms of an identity or even victim politics, to third-wave feminisms. In part, because her oeuvre demonstrates the predicament of straddling discrete but separate waves of feminism, her novels merit the kind of close scrutiny and reappraisal that I undertake in this book.

Chapter 1 analyses the resistance to autobiography as a genre in Shields's early novels and locates her in a growing tradition of women's life writing since the 1970s. The early works are autobiographical and confessional but they are also metafictional. In *Small Ceremonies* biographer Judith Gill keeps a journal while researching the life of novelist Susanna Moodie, and in *The Box Garden* poet Charleen Forrest writes a travel journal while seeking and eventually rejecting her modernist and masculine mentor. In the former novel, Shields constructs a series of mises en abyme to self-reflexively challenge generic boundaries and to produce a resisting reading of the autobiographical pact characterized by Lejeune. In the latter novel, Shields constructs an alternative discourse on the self to present a feminine "metaphysic of survival" (213), not a metaphysics of presence. Charleen's confession presents a gendered self, an interconnected self, and a discursive self. Both novels create their political effects by valorizing women's autobiographical production and inscribing intersubjectivity, particularly when read together as portraying interconnected subjects.

Chapter 2, on *Swann*, re-examines the relationship between author and text with regard to Michel Foucault's question: what is an author? Poet Mary Swann is transformed posthumously into an "author" by her publisher, critics, biographer, and bookseller; and she becomes a model of author-construction, which is characterized by a process of attribution, appropriation, circulation, and, eventually, valorization. The process is complicated by the epitaph of *victim* because of her murder at the hand of a jealous spouse, a plot by which Shields alludes to Pat Lowther, a Canadian poet and victim of a rivalrous husband. The victim is a gender stereotype, as a comparison of Swann's and Lowther's lives demonstrates. Swann is appropriated not only to romantic, but also feminist, realist, modernist, and nationalist discourses, and the author disappears. More importantly, Swann is marginalized as a lost female writer, just as Lowther's work is obscured by the label of a victim. Shields gives a reconstructed life both an ironic twist and a feminist twist. Swann's story reads like a cautionary tale about her exclusion from literary and critical practices. Shields writes against the grain in a feminist critique of dominant representations of women writers, while revealing the material effects of interpretive communities. At the same time, Shields's narrative models an ethical discourse by commemorating Swann – and Lowther. The author-construction in the discourse of critics is satirized, even as Foucault's discourse is parodied, but the woman writer is valorized.

Chapter 3 considers the problem of the body by examining the ways in which the romantic novel becomes a model for curator and critic Fay McLeod's self-representations. In *The Republic of Love* the romantic discourse of literary and popular culture calls her as a subject, beckoning like a mermaid, while corresponding not to the real, but to a Baudrillardian hyperreal. Like her quixotic father, she derives from reading a desire to be a romantic heroine in her own life story. The romantic discourse is exposed as a metaphysical ruin. But her autobiographical discourse is embedded in a metafiction that reinscribes the body as the grounds for an inquiry into the relationship between identity and representation. Fay still confuses a "precession of the model" (Baudrillard 32) with the "particularity" of her sexual desire for Tom (*Republic* 364). She sees romance as her destiny, until she encounters resistance from her middle-class family to Tom's working-class origins. She confronts her multiple identities as a daughter, lover, and critic, revealing intersecting identities defined by gender and class. She breaks off her engagement to Tom, but she can neither sleep without nor forget the memory of his body. Coinciding with these events is her research for a book on mermaids as gender stereotypes. Like bodies, artefacts become intrusions of the real into the hyperreal. Abrupt reversals in Fay's life transform her writing by challenging her critical assumptions. A series of crises – including her godmother's loss of a long-time lover and her parents' break-up and reunion – precipitates Fay's return to Tom by prostrating herself at his door. A marriage ceremony and book launch demand a performative subject and her writing becomes a social and political act. The reversal and re-reversal of the romantic plot create a narrative fold and feminist double strategy, by which Shields emphasizes an intersubjectivity to subvert cultural discourses of desire and individualism.

Chapter 4 analyses how the multiple-voiced narration of *The Stone Diaries* interrogates the autobiographical subject, as well as the text's status as autobiography or biography. By resisting both genres it reads as a feminist critique. A significant detail that escapes critical attention shapes this reading: the epigraph is written not by Daisy Goodwill, but by Judith Downing. Taken from the poem "The Grandmother Cycle," the epigraph characterizes Daisy as a woman who never said "quite what she meant" but whose life "could be called a monument." The quotation becomes a framing device to transform the narrative into a text that problematizes autobiography and historiography. As Daisy contemplates her life story, an unnamed I-narrator reports that she feels as though she were part of an "apocryphal journal" (118). The unauthorized biography in which Daisy's life is embedded dramatizes Virginia Woolf's notion that we think back through our mothers if we are women. To compile an alternative history is the project of Judith who, in collaboration with her mother and family, rewrites her grandmother's life. The text's genre is indeterminate and presents a game with the reader. The narrative is best read as an apocryphal history, which, according to Brian McHale (90–1), seeks to restore women's lives to the historical record. The unnamed narrator's term "apocryphal journal" is indeed apt because the resistance of gender stereotypes emerges as the structuring principle of the narrative. *The Stone Diaries* is a complex, theoretical novel that paradoxically produces both postmodernist and feminist readings of the autobiographical subject and genre.

Chapter 5 discusses the problem of the subject of feminism as an object of inquiry in *Unless*. The autobiography of novelist Reta Winters distracts her from the crisis of a runaway daughter, who lives in silence on the streets of Toronto. The present crisis decentres a writing subject that is parodically exposed and performative: it is constituted in not only feminist discourses, but also Western discourses of individualism. From the "Freedom chair" of her middle-class suburban home (64), Reta's writing reveals the limited perspective and political interestedness of her liberal ideology and identity politics. While tracing her own development in her journal and fiction, Reta cannot understand her daughter's struggle or the related struggle of a Saudi woman. Reta's use of the category of *woman* erases differences of class and race, as Judith Butler might say, and as the unfolding and enfolding embedded narratives reveal. All of Reta's explanatory narratives fail and many gaps remain at the end of her journal, despite the supposed discovery of the cause for Norah's silence. The implication of the mother and daughter, and by extension the reader, in a Muslim woman's self-immolation raises incendiary political and ethical questions. The open ending creates a torsion of the narrative into ambivalence and frustrates the reader's expectation of the discovery of self-perception. Shields depicts the feminist subject as neither stable nor autonomous, but rather historical and provisional. Shields makes space for rethinking the subject of feminism as collective and global and for rediscovering the movement's liberating potential.

In this book I examine, then, a series of issues that form the critical and theoretical concerns of Shields's fiction in relation to women's autobiographical practices: the problem of the genre, the problem of the author, the problem of the body, the problem of the subject, and the problem of the subject of feminism. These issues are addressed in relation to the novels in chronological order to demonstrate the development of Shields's political project over her career as a novelist. The historical period that is represented by her work is important for spanning transformative shifts in emergent feminisms of recent decades after the Women's Movement in the 1960s and 1970s, and for intersecting with a cultural paradigm shift from critical theory to theory that emphasizes political and ethical practices. The reception of Shields's work has, to some degree, been adversely affected by these cultural shifts. She has, on the one hand, been praised for an attention to women's lives; and she has, on the other hand, been dismissed for an emphasis on domesticity. At the same time, she has been disregarded for a familiar Canadian realism and ignored for a postmodern irony or excessive playfulness. Instead, her work must be regarded as successfully negotiating the rock and a hard place of both critical debates, though not without tensions. But the criticism of Shields largely ignores the complexity and subtlety of her evolving feminist critique. As a prime example of women's activism in a supposedly post-feminist age, her work remains urgent and ready for critical reassessment.

In the autobiographical labyrinths of her narratives, Shields interrogates and performs the most relevant of theoretical and political manoeuvres. The self-representation and narrated lives of women writers become almost hyperreal. They read as simulations of a real life but are designed for a political purpose: to rewrite a feminist critique of literary history and critical thought. The multi-voicedness and mixed genres of Shields's ficto-criticism, while distancing both author and reader from the main character, generate an interactive space inside and outside the text. A popular and award-winning novelist, Shields reaches the broad audience that is demonstrated by recent editions of her work in French, Spanish, Italian, Portuguese, and Finnish as well as English. In the hazardous labyrinth that is the autobiographical space, Shields creates a space for readers to rethink social and ethical relations. In these ways, her novels are written against the grain of autobiography in order to expose the specular structure of the genre, and the limits of both the genre and critical theory to represent female subjects. With a wry and self-conscious voice, Shields makes even the subject of feminism an object of inquiry for the purpose of reinscribing a cultural critique from the historical and political perspectives of women writers.

Chapter One

The Problem of the Genre:
The Autobiographical Pact in
Small Ceremonies and *The Box Garden*

Carol Shields's early works, *Small Ceremonies* (1976) and *The Box Garden* (1977), begin the troubling of genre that is apparent in all of her novels. They draw attention to the problem of the genre of autobiography, particularly the crossing of boundaries between fiction and non-fiction. Both early works are written in the first person from the perspective of a woman writer – biographer Judith Gill and poet Charleen Forrest, respectively – with a focus on the writing process itself and the material production of a text as viewed from a feminine perspective. Both works ostensibly take the autobiographical form of a journal: Judith's covers nine months like a diary, and Charleen's covers one week like a travel journal. With nine chapters representing nine months from September to May, *Small Ceremonies* suggests a gestation period in which Judith also births the biography of Susanna Moodie. Wendy Roy remarks that Shields's later work "turns autobiography into critical practice by engaging with feminist theories of life writing" ("Autobiography" 114), an insight that equally applies to her early work.[1] Critics cannot agree on a term for Shields's novels, precisely because the genre of autobiography is problematized by the embedded life narratives throughout her oeuvre. Neither *Small Ceremonies* nor *The Box Garden* is as conventional in form as it first appears. Shields mixes autobiography, fiction, and criticism in such a way that even the early novels must be read as complex autobiographical metafictions.

Central to Shields's early works is a sophisticated play on the autobiographical pact as defined by French theorist Philippe Lejeune, an early critic in the field. Lejeune initially defines autobiography as a "retrospective prose narrative written by a real person concerning his own existence, where the focus is his individual life, in particular the story of his personality" or identity ("Pact" 4). While his characterization of the term appears to exclude women and fiction, Lejeune goes on to deconstruct the definition. He subsequently defines autobiography not as a genre, but as a mode of reading that is historically variable. He distinguishes autobiography from biography and the autobiographical novel by the "autobiographical pact" (13). This pact is a social contract, which refers to the author's signature on the title page as a guarantee that the author, narrator, and protagonist are one and the same; therefore, he regards the autobiographical mode as a narrative effect or reading practice and not a distinct genre. While ultimately insisting on the impossibility of defining autobiography, Lejeune still considers the term useful: "It is through their elasticity, their plasticity, their polysemy, that literary terms (like others) promote dialogue and ensure the continuity of language" ("Bis" 122). Following this line of thinking, he uses "autobiography" to "designate broadly any text governed by an autobiographical pact, in which an author proposes to the reader a discourse on the self" (124). His view suggests that a broad spectrum of autobiographical practices is possible.

Shields's early works fall within this spectrum in their emphasis on the social contract and discourses on the self. At the same time, they introduce an element that is missing from Lejeune's redefinition: a critical reconsideration of the role that ideology plays in life writing.[2] From the outset of her career, Shields's novels can be viewed as ideological acts that address the politics of self-representation through the life stories of their female narrators. Because women's voices are too often silenced, these texts perform the type of critique that is identified by feminist theorists such as Leigh Gilmore and Sidonie Smith to discuss the politics of self-representation. Shields self-reflexively dramatizes the autobiographical pact in *Small Ceremonies* to complicate and resist autobiography, and she creates an alternative discourse on the self in *The Box Garden*. By employing the self-reflexive techniques of the mise en abyme and parody, Shields undermines unspoken gender ideologies that marginalize women's autobiographical and biographical production.

In *Small Ceremonies*, Shields creates a series of embedded texts or mises en abyme. A woman writer's representation of the life of another woman writer – Shields's writing about Judith who is writing about Moodie – is only one level of the text's mises en abyme.[3]

In this instance it would be only a simple duplication. By Jeremy Hawthorn's definition, an effective use of the mises en abyme would be the complex and "recurring internal duplication of images of an artistic whole, such that an infinite series of images disappearing into invisibility is produced – similar to what one witnesses if one looks at one's reflection between two facing mirrors" (210). In Shields the notion of infinite regress evokes Lejeune's concept of the impossibility of defining autobiography. It is significant that Shields's earliest novel is structured by a series of embedded texts that cast doubt on identity and originality, at least in Judith's mind as she reads male authors including John Spalding and Furlong Eberhardt. The pact with the reader is thereby disrupted, subverting the expectation that the author, narrator, and protagonist are identical.

The first embedded text is Spalding's unpublished novel, which Judith discovers while living at his home on a sabbatical leave in England. Spalding's first-person narrative portrays a "sensitive young man" on a "journey between wretchedness and joy and back to wretchedness" (37).[4] The novel of development is a conventional form in the autobiographical mode, yet Judith finds in it "a plot of fairly breathless originality" and speculates whether he had "lived this plot himself" (37). In other words, the narrator, like any autobiographer, asks, "Who is 'I?'" ("Pact" 8), emphasizing the discursive subject. This question raises the problem of the author, since the use of the first person "has reference only in its own enunciation" ("Pact" 10). When Judith discovers Spalding's diary, his confessions seem to confirm her autobiographical reading that the author is the "tormented hero" (38). She admits that "he reached me" and "his terrible sorrowing stayed with me" (39). Judith characterizes Spalding's text as an autobiographical novel; and she, like any reader of autobiography, "has reason to suspect, from the resemblances that [s]he thinks [s]he sees, that there is an identity of author and *protagonist*" ("Pact" 13; original emphasis). But the novel form itself denies the author-narrator-protagonist identity. The novel is governed by a "fictional pact" rather than an autobiographical pact; nevertheless, the reader "will attempt to establish resemblances, in spite of the author" ("Pact" 14). The autobiographical novel includes personal narratives and it plays upon the ambiguity of the narrator-protagonist's identity: "Autobiography is a literary genre which, by its very content, best marks the confusion of author and person, confusion on which is founded the whole practice and problematic of Western literature since the end of the eighteenth century" ("Pact" 20). With keen irony, Shields's text signals a self-consciousness about this history in *Small Ceremonies*.[5]

The second embedded text is *The Magic Rocking Horse*, Judith's unpublished novel, which she writes for a creative writing class after she returns from England. Struggling with writer's block, she decides to "borrow" Spalding's plot, which she once found so original (71). Her "plagiarism" raises again the problem of identity as a discursive construct. In an obvious attempt at self-justification her mind strays towards Renaissance painters: "It had been a less arrogant age in which creativity had been shared; surely that was an ennobling precedent. For I didn't intend anything as crude as stealing John Spalding's plot outright ... All I needed to borrow was the underlying plot structure" (71). Judith casts doubt on the originality of self-expression by tracing it to a romantic aesthetic and the discourses of presence and beauty that have dominated art since the Renaissance. Her reflections recall other critiques that show that originality is equated with identity and opposed to reproduction (Benjamin 224). In spite of herself, she believes she has reproduced Spalding's text, and withdraws her manuscript. Judith urges her instructor, "Burn it. Tear it up" (73). She retracts any pact, autobiographical or fictional, and resolves instead to write only biography, because she thinks that fiction is a web of lies. She admits, "I found the essential silliness of make-believe disturbing" (66–7). Even in her work she expects clear distinctions between fact and fiction. This view will not be challenged until Judith encounters an autobiographical novel by Moodie, the subject of her biography.

The third embedded text is *Graven Images*, Eberhardt's best-selling novel. Judith is outraged because she thinks that Eberhardt has plagiarized her manuscript. She feels betrayed because of a perceived violation of the autobiographical pact. She thinks the text is autobiographical in its origin with Spalding and it shatters her expectation of the author-narrator-protagonist identity. She confuses the notion of identity with that of resemblance, which is the domain of the novel. *Graven Images* becomes a complex mise en abyme that involves more than a simple duplication:

So simply, so transparently, and so unapologetically had he stolen the plot for *Graven Images* – stolen it from me who had in turn stolen it from

John Spalding who – it occurred to me for the first time – might have stolen it from someone else. The chain of indictment might stretch back infinitely, crime within crime within crime. (105–6)

Eberhardt's novel functions self-reflexively as a mirror text,[6] because it exposes the infinite regress and endless deferral of meaning among words regardless of who uses them. As such, the novel reveals the problem of authorship. *Graven Images* could be considered a *"transcendental mise en abyme,"* for it reveals that "the originating reality" is "by definition out of reach" (Dällenbach 101; original emphasis). In the context of Shields's novel, *Graven Images* provides a "narrativizing of the problematics of its own writing"; consequently, it is best considered a *"metatextual mise en abyme"* (Dällenbach 98; original emphasis). Like Judith's unpublished novel, it calls into question a romantic aesthetic that is located outside the text.

After Judith labels him a swine for stealing her plot, Eberhardt recalls in his own defence a traditional aesthetic theory that predates the Romantic period and its doctrine of self-expression:

> Where did Shakespeare get his plots? Not from his own experience, you can be sure of that. I mean, who was he but another young lad from the provinces? He stole his plots, you would say, Judith. Borrowed them from the literature of the past, and no one damn well calls it theft. He took those old tried and true stories and hammered them into something that was his own. (131–2)

Eberhardt's text reproduces literary conventions that generate, in Benjamin's words, a novel's "aura" and an author's "presence" (221). Fictional conventions are so naturalized by repeated use that they can create an effect of the real. Judith appears to be persuaded by Eberhardt's argument, for she does not pursue the charge of plagiarism. She realizes that with her manuscript "it had not been the thought of plagiarism that had deterred me, but rather the inability to reconcile the real with the unreal" (106). Judith must acknowledge that a novel, such as *Graven Images*, cannot violate the autobiographical pact because it establishes a fictional pact with the reader. When Judith discovers later at the Immigration Department that Furlong Eberhardt is a pseudonym for Rudyard Eberhardt and that the celebrated Canadian writer is actually American-born (154), she still does not expose his identity. Evidently, her opinion approaches Lejeune's view:

> A pseudonym is a name that is different from the one found in vital statistics, which a real person uses in order to *publish* all or part of his writings. The pseudonym is the name of an *author*. It is not exactly a false name, but a pen name ... and almost never [associated] with a work being passed off as the autobiography of an *author*. Literary pseudonyms are in general neither mysteries nor hoaxes. ("Pact" 12; original emphasis)

She suspends her judgment about him, just as she does about the distinctions between fact and fiction.

Besides the play with metatextual mises en abyme, Shields provides another way of reading the "real" within her novel, one that can be understood in relation to the "cultural production of a politics of identity, a politics that maintains identity hierarchies through its reproduction of class, sexuality, race, and gender" (Gilmore, "Mark" 5). In contrast to Eberhardt's supposedly masculine (though gay) and stable identity as an author, Judith's feminine identity includes the multiple identities of wife, mother, and writer. In addition to writing, she performs mundane tasks such as making meals: "The clatter of cutlery, a knife pulling down on a wooden board, an onion halved showing rings of pearl; their distinct and separate clarity thrilled me. This was real" (73). Her admission reveals the divided self of a woman who is caught between competing identities of feminine self-effacement and literary or masculine ambition. Judith perceives that she has been limited by her perspective and insistence upon distinct categories of "real" and "unreal," "fact" and "fiction." Eberhardt's success contrasts with Judith's failure as a novelist and she feels envy: "I didn't actually go through with it [writing a novel]. And I didn't profit from it the way Furlong has profited" (113). She suspends her judgment of him but not without resistance: "There is something I have not quite managed to assimilate" (132). A gap of knowledge signals a gap in the dominant discourse – that is, an ideological gap or assumption. What she knows, if only subconsciously, is that even her identity as an author of non-fiction is culturally subordinated to an author of literature, although her identity as a biographer is invested with some social power: "All sorts of people, in fact, whom I know in a remote and professional way began using my first name the moment my first book came out, as though I had somehow come into the inheritance of it, as though I had entered into the public domain, had left behind that dumpy housewife, Mrs Gill. *Judith*. I became Judith" (91; original emphasis). She recognizes that the social categories and values assigned to authorship are in practice related to genre and gender.

In a fourth embedded text Judith becomes increasingly aware of gender ideologies. In her biography of the novelist Susanna Moodie, she begins to see autobiographical discourse as a site of identity production and resistance. She observes Moodie's conflicting gender roles as wife, mother, and writer; moreover, she discovers the gaps in her subject's story. Moodie omits details about her sexual life by scarcely mentioning the "bridal bed" (33). Judith notices the writer's silence about "her rage against the husband" who, as an immigrant farmer, "gave her a rough shanty to live in." Judith marvels at Moodie's "Victorian restraint": she did not "crow when her royalty cheques came in, proclaiming herself the household saviour" (6–7). Moodie rescues her family from debt by writing a letter to the lieutenant-governor to have her husband reinstated in the militia, but she maintains a delicate silence by keeping it secret from her husband. An imbalance of power based on gender is also reflected in the couple's names; she goes by her personal name while she calls her husband by his public or family name. As Judith reads these ideological gaps, she becomes increasingly aware of a cultural politics of identity, with distinct differences among men and women being defined in terms of social hierarchies. The socially imposed limits of representation, particularly gender ideologies, are exposed in Moodie's writing, despite the feminine stance of courtesy or decency that "shimmers beneath her prose" (6). In Moodie's autobiographical novel, *Flora Lindsay*, Judith discerns an implicit self-representation as a heroine: "Flora is refined, virtuous, bright, lively, humorous: her only fault is an occasional pout when her husband places some sort of restraint on her" (153). In her book Moodie reproduces a cultural fiction about feminine virtue, silence, and self-effacement – a common rhetorical strategy of women before the twentieth century to establish their narrative authority (S. Smith 54). Ironically, Shields suggests that less has changed in one hundred fifty years than one might think. Judith regards Moodie's text as a "projection, a view of herself," an "idealized picture" of her life story that reinscribes an ideology of gender (152–3). At the same time, Judith interprets

Moodie's irony as a mark of resistance and an example of her social action. Moodie creates a double-voicedness that characterizes women's autobiographical production, even before the twentieth century.

Judith's representations of Moodie are projections of herself onto the biographical subject: "I easily recognize the nuances of irony because ... I too do my balancing act between humour and desperation" (123). Early in her research Judith claims to have found "a kindred spirit" (6), and she seeks to create in her narrative portrait "a delicate design which may just possibly be the real Susanna" (7). Later she is less certain: "Did Susanna really see herself that way?" (153). When Judith sends her biography to the publisher, she is still uncertain about the accuracy of her narrative. Judith recognizes that her representation is historical and provisional, not fixed. Like the other embedded texts, the biography of Moodie challenges the boundaries between fact and fiction – and the boundaries between biography and autobiography. The distinctions between genres begin to blur and Judith comes to realize that "biography is the least exact of the sciences" (53). She attempts to ground in archival research the narrative portrait of a secret self, as Leon Edel urges biographers to do (34). But the biographer, much like the novelist, remains a storyteller. Judith writes autobiographically while creating her portrait of Moodie. Biography becomes a form of self-writing from the narrator's perspective.

On another level, the mise en abyme of Shields's writing about Judith, who is writing about Moodie, who is writing about Flora, challenges the boundaries of autobiographical discourse from the reader's perspective. The real author of *Small Ceremonies* is also the critic and author of *Susanna Moodie: Voice and Vision*. Intriguingly, Shields left in her own archive a copy of Leon Edel's seminal article on biography; it is dated 12 February 1985 and signed simply for Carol, "who, I am told, likes biography" (LMS-0212 1994–13 69, f. 12).[7] In fact, Shields deliberately blurs generic boundaries by stating elsewhere that the material that was left over from her Master's thesis on Moodie became her first novel (Shields, qtd. in Wachtel, "Interview" 27). With this novel, Shields the critic, in effect, rereads the autobiographical pact.

The mises en abyme that involve three writers, Moodie, Eberhardt, and Spalding, are all embedded in Judith's journal. In fact, Shields's text includes still another series of mises en abyme. Three more mirror texts function as metafictional and indirect commentaries to reflect the development of Judith's self-perception and awareness of gender ideologies. These mirror texts appear at the beginning, middle, and end of her journal. At the beginning, Judith and her family are watching a television documentary about the mating practices of a rare bird. Ironically, the host is "speaking in a low voice" and his gestures towards the bird are solicitous: "He is leaning over, and his hands, very gentle, very sensitive, attach a slender identification tag to the leg of a tiny bird. The bird shudders in his hand" (4). The documentary's narrative naturalizes gender relations that are monogamous and heterosexual; its ideological message is that they are necessary to survival. The supposedly objective voice of the host implies that the bird's fixed habits of finding a new mate every year are the reason for its species' endangered status. The anthropomorphizing narrative is not lost on Judith: "Every year a new mate; it is beyond imagining." Her teenaged daughter insists the bird's courtship ritual is romantic and "beautiful" (4), but her adolescent son resists the notion: "It's a dumb program anyway" (3). Each family member is positioned as a gendered subject by the nature documentary's popular discourse, though Judith seems almost unconscious of its ideological effects.

In the middle of her journal, Judith is troubled by a tapestry that her husband weaves to represent intersecting themes in Milton's *Paradise Lost*. It is not his hiding the tapestry and wool that disturbs Judith, but rather his apparent confusion of gender roles. Martin's mother knits and Judith associates wool with Lala's femininity. Like his father, Martin is an academic who assumes the so-called masculine roles of teaching and writing, not knitting and weaving:

> "I can't bear to think of you sitting there in your office weaving away. I mean ... don't you think it's just a little bit – you know – ?"
>
> "Effeminate?" he supplies the word. (86)

So naturalized are her assumptions about gender that Judith cannot answer the question, "What am I afraid of?" (86). Her discovery of his tapestry precipitates the central crisis of her journal. Under stress she catches the flu, signalling an ideological crisis and shift in perception. Even after her recovery, the tapestry represents "something obscurely humiliating" (139). To her surprise, Martin's project is praised by peers while three galleries offer to purchase it and a collector buys it for "a sizable sum" (177). The anonymous buyer is probably Martin's colleague, Eberhardt, who has promised to do Judith a good turn for giving him the idea for his recent novel. Like Moodie, she is indirectly and secretly responsible for advancing her husband's career.

At the end of Judith's journal, a final mirror text is the sign language that Judith and Martin see performed by the hearing-impaired at the restaurant where diners rejoice over Martin's success. Despite the silence of their signing, Judith is struck by the communicative gesture. It is inclusive regardless of the participants' gender. It is also provisional and dynamic as part of "the larger stories of their separate lives" (179). Sign language offers a communication model that Judith – and by extension Shields – favours by the end as a way of understanding even literary discourse. As Wallace Martin remarks on the nature of narrative:

> Perhaps the creation of meaning is a cooperative enterprise, reader and writer both contributing a share; possibly the real determinants of interpretation are the literary and cultural assumptions of particular communities in history, since these shape what writers and readers perceive and create. (156)

Autobiographical discourse can be understood, too, in the contexts of a "history of literary *communication*" and modes of reading (Lejeune, "Pact" 30; original emphasis). With an evolving critical context and communication model for narrative discourse, the mise en abyme of signing becomes a self-reflexive trope for women's storytelling, including Judith's and Shields's, in the late twentieth century.

In the context of communication, Martin's tapestry requires rethinking by Judith because it challenges the boundaries of gender codes and generic codes. Jacques Derrida makes the connection between genre and gender: "the semantic scale of *genre* [in French] is much larger and more expansive than in English, and thus always includes within its reach ... gender" (74). Martin's work tests the limits of the genres that are available for critique. The tapestry functions as a critical trope for narrative and a metatextual mise en abyme:

> The emblematic metaphor of the text as "fabric" reactivates the etymology of the "text" ... It is a *topos* ... text and textiles both being interwoven – hence the frequent use of terms like "web," "embroidering" and "weaving" to describe the novelist's work – both constituting a *texture*,

i.e., an interlinked arrangement of elements, a relational network, or, if
one prefers, a *structure*. (Dällenbach 96; original emphasis)

Shields uses the tapestry self-consciously to suggest the arbitrariness
of gender codes and to promote the mixing of genres.

Throughout the text Shields subtly and deliberately mixes genres
for the purpose of embedding a peculiarly feminist critique. Because
women's self-writing presumably "belongs to some 'homelier' and
minor traditions" including the letter, diary, and journal (Gilmore, *Autobiographics* 1–2), its reception is uncertain. Judith's journal
encompasses the saleable works of Martin, Eberhardt, and Spalding, yet her text remains unpublished. The irony is heightened by
Spalding's announcement that his latest novel, which is based on the
experiences of Judith's family, will be published as *Alien Interlude*.
Rather than seeing his book as plagiarized, Judith eventually sees
that all "writers use material selectively" (175). She takes a broader
view in the end than she did earlier in her account: "I have seen
how facts are transmuted as they travel through a series of hands ...
[from] letter-writing prose ... [to] publisher – surely by the time it
reaches print, the least dram of truth will be drained away" (176).
But by embedding Eberhardt's and Spalding's texts in Judith's journal, Shields validates Judith's work and effectively reverses the hierarchies of genre and gender.

The material that is publishable as a novel by Eberhardt remains
unpublishable as a journal by Judith, at least intratextually. Extra-
textually, *Small Ceremonies* is published and it is Judith Gill's book
(Shields, qtd. in De Roo 44–5), blurring the boundaries between
autobiography and the novel. By creating irony and generic ambiguity, Shields produces in Judith's journal a resistant reading of the
autobiographical pact, in order to question why only a male author's
signature guarantees an authorized discourse of truth and identity.
In *Small Ceremonies*, the aim of the metafictional mise en abyme is
to change the world for women's writing by changing its reception.
Shields offers more than a postmodern critique that is sceptical of
genre; her narrative is a political act that asserts women's right to
publish their autobiographical and hybrid discourses. The novelist
makes visible what Leigh Gilmore describes as "the unequal positioning of persons in relation to the autobiographical pact" (*Autobiographics* 50–1). Thus, Shields generates a feminist critique by
employing self-reflexivity in *Small Ceremonies* to the degree that it

becomes a form of resistance. The novel's parody extends beyond the covers of the book, and Shields positions herself among the best of Canadian writers who have "teased the life/art borders of self-consciously autobiographical fiction" (Hutcheon, *Canadian* 87). As Shields's parody shows, the literary field is contained within a broader field of power (Bourdieu 37). Her parodic and self-reflexive strategies expose the implication of genre in a social privileging of men's writing over women's writing. Like Judith, the reader is called to rethink the categories of fact and fiction.

Shields's political project continues in *The Box Garden* even though she labels it the "one book I would recall if I could" (Shields, qtd. in Anderson 144). She regrets her capitulation to an editor who regarded her plot as slow, a critical view that resulted in the addition of a "pseudo kidnapping" (Shields, qtd. in Wachtel, "Interview" 32). But a concession to editorial demands does not mar her purpose in this case, although the disclaimer may account for the novel's critical neglect. An embedded parody of crime fiction, which Gretta reads and Charleen watches on television's *Hawaii Five-O* (176), heightens the novel's postmodern critique by mixing genres of popular culture with high culture. More importantly, the novel's feminist critique of the subordination of women writers to the mediators of cultural production, such as editors, is underlined by the struggles of the protagonist and the author herself in her life and fiction. In terms of the material production of the text, her embedded critique once again carries implications beyond the covers of the book. Shields presents in this novel a cultural critique of Western metaphysics, particularly the autonomous male self. In opposition to a metaphysics of presence, the novel proposes a feminine "metaphysic of survival" (*Box* 213). The autobiographical narrative of poet and copy-editor Charleen Forrest becomes a conscious discourse on the self. In a search for self-transformation that is typical of literary confessions, Charleen also resists the notion of the autonomous self that is represented by her narcissistic ex-husband, Watson Forrest. Her journal, while spanning only one week, becomes a kind of alternative autobiography; it models the self-writing by which women challenge dominant masculine discourses of identity and presence. Charleen's journal represents a gendered self, an interconnected self, and a discursive self.

Charleen describes herself initially as a single mother and she works part-time as a copy-editor for an academic quarterly, *The*

National Botanical Journal. Although she enjoys a reputation as a poet, she is "more clerk than poet" (20). Like Judith, she works primarily with non-fiction. Her editor, Doug Savage, hired Charleen as the "bereft wife of his former friend" and founding editor. She calls herself a "thirty-eight-year-old divorcée who knows nothing about botany and who has no training beyond high school," and her position is undefined although her "need for cash is absolute and recurring" (11–12). Charleen cannot afford to maintain the "disinterestedness" that legitimates poetry: the disavowal of the economy that a critic might say is "at the very heart" of the field of cultural production (Bourdieu 79). She lives in a small three-room apartment, wearing "falling-apart skirts" and eating day-old bread, to support her son, Seth, on minimal child support and a small salary (1–2). Her daily life is defined by a cubicle where "the lack of a lock and key seems to underscore the valuelessness of what I do" (15). In contrast, the editor's office has a locking door. As a botanist he is "defined by his specialty," for which he is rewarded with tenure even though Charleen does almost everything (20). Doug enjoys a large house in New Westminster, meals in restaurants, and wine and crêpes at home despite his disavowal of middle-class values. If Charleen is aware of a lower-middle-class upbringing in a Scarborough bungalow, she is even more aware of a gendered body, which needs deliverance from ex-husbands and "men on the make who want her to lie back and accept (this is what you need, baby)" (3). Her journal reveals contesting discourses – narratives of "'erotic' and 'ambitious' plots" in the life of a woman writer (Buss, "Abducting" 435) – to show the limited self-representational models that are available to the women of her time.

Charleen's low-paid work is a material consequence of a gendered body that is implicated in her identity. Doug calls her "angel, sweetheart, love, baby" while she calls him "Bossman" (16–17). Although she resists her subordination by ironically affecting a southern drawl, Charleen indeed occupies a subordinate position in the field of cultural production. Her position at the journal shows that the literary field is not autonomous; it is contained within both the field of power, including gender relations, and the field of class relations (Bourdieu 37–8). Significantly, Charleen's job reflects Shields's first job as an editorial assistant for the quarterly *Canadian Slavonic Papers,* a "jobette" that nonetheless meant a great deal to her (Shields, qtd. in Wachtel, "Interview" 26–7). Even Shields's subsequent position as a sessional lecturer was only part-time with "temporary office space" (Buss, "Abducting" 435). With echoes that extend well beyond the book's covers, Shields's fictional and autobiographical representation of a woman writer is just as political in *The Box Garden* as in *Small Ceremonies*. The gendered self is economically and socially disadvantaged.

Along with low pay, another material effect of Charleen's identity as a single mother is the loss of a house in upscale West Vancouver. As an "abandoned woman" (11), Charleen cannot afford the home where she and Watson lived comfortably with neat hedges "shaped into startled spheres" and flowers in "nicely-painted window boxes" (14). She walks alone past her old house on afternoons that are reserved for writing poetry. As a young woman she fell away from middle-class respectability to become a bohemian and runaway daughter; she had "eloped with a student" and "ridden off to Vancouver on the back of a motorcycle" (142). As a middle-aged woman she is again seen as a fallen woman, the "semi-mistress" of Eugene Redding (78). Female desire can be understood as transgressive but Charleen records only the pleasure of "his hand on my bare thighs" during a train trip home: "I sit still, half-drowning in a stirring helium happiness" (66). Still, she struggles with her complex relationship to gendered figures of the self: the journal emphasizes not only her marginalized position, but also her lack of authority in relation to a gendered body and identity.

Charleen's writing does not demonstrate the unitary self that is produced by a traditional literary autobiography, but a subject that is multiple and contradictory. Gilmore observes that women's lives are often characterized by interruption, fragmentation, and discontinuity, and that "the search for a way to represent this instability forms the grounds of autobiographical experimentation" (*Autobiographics* 26). Charleen plays the role of a confessor who laments her abandonment by Watson and contemplates a second marriage. She confesses to Eugene a sense of lack: "There's nothing about myself that I like" (35). At the same time, she is weary of self-hatred. The urgency of her self-examination is heightened by a series of crises, including the return home for her mother's remarriage, the approach of mid-life, and a secret desire for reunion with the absent Watson. But Charleen finds in Eugene a ready interlocutor with whom she can discuss the mystery of sex and shared self-perceptions as "victims of failed marriages" (52). Historical forces, such as the Women's Movement, have reshaped their personal histories (41). For Charleen, who lacks social authority, life writing provides the means of self-definition, whereas literary autobiography produces and polices ideas about truth, gender, and identity. Women's self-writing can be used to authorize new identities and this is the aim of Shields's use of the first person in Charleen's journal.

In addition to being a gendered self, Charleen is represented as an interconnected self. As a poet Charleen has developed her writing skills not in a vacuum, but under Watson's mentorship. Watson taught her to write modern poetry influenced by T.S. Eliot,[8] but Charleen thinks of such poetry as an artifice: "painstakingly assembled, an artificial montage of poetic parts" and "dark-edged metaphors" (151–2). She became disillusioned after penning new poems about her abandonment: while the lines were more original, critics failed to distinguish them from her early work. Their characterization of "the arresting Charleen Forrest," as though she were one "seamless whole" (152), reveals the underlying ideology of a unified self that she perceives as false. This ideology, like Watson's modernism, is grounded in the assumption of an autonomous and masculine self. Watson professes literary and liberal values of individualism and freedom. By contrast, Charleen sees that she is culturally defined by a woman's lack: even the maiden name McNinn evokes "nothing, non-entity, nobody" (3). From a humble position she admits, "The truth is, I am a sort of phony poet; poetry was grafted artificially onto my lazy unconnectedness, and it was Watson ... who did the grafting" (150). Charleen regards with irony the "pome people," her contemporaries who pose as "sensitivity machines" only to manufacture lyrics that are highly derivative (60). Symbolism and dreams are their currency, just as Watson is "big on symbols" (94, 109). These poets promote an inverse relationship between profit and prestige. Poetry stands at the top of the hierarchy of genres above fiction and non-fiction, at least in Watson's mind. In his perpetuation of "youth cult hash" (94), he embodies "the priority accorded to 'youth' and to the associated values of change and originality" (Bourdieu 105). Charleen's journal promotes not an individual selfhood, with its presumed autonomy and originality, but communal figures of selfhood and interconnection.

Even Watson moves towards communal life on a small farm. Charleen says that he had one nervous breakdown at thirty that destroyed his marriage and another at forty that drove him from his commune. Charleen confesses to Judith that Watson's initial crisis precipitated her own. Charleen measures herself against the standard of romantic and autonomous selfhood. She berates herself for a perceived lack of courage or self-determination by asking, "Why can't I learn to be brave?" (98). She sees her elder sister as "brave, kind, curious Judith" (111), but she judges herself harshly: "I will never be brave" (1). This conflict emerges not in her poetry but in her journal. As Sidonie Smith asserts, courage, intelligence, and energy are often sought by women but associated with "the power, authority, and voice of a man"; in women's autobiography these traits are contrasted with constraint, confusion, and ambivalence (62). A masculine genre is the probable cause of Charleen's writer's block. She dabbles with autobiographical poetry but in two years she has "hardly written a line" (12). By writing a journal instead she moves from writer's block to renewed creativity. In an open and confessional form new self-perception and insights erupt. Even Watson's masculine selfhood is not regarded as unitary in her journal; rather, it is a "life hacked to pieces by his endless self-regarding" (201). Charleen seeks not autonomy but interconnection.

Reconnecting with Judith at her mother's house, Charleen confesses that she left Watson primarily because of what her mother would think if she took her son, Seth, to live like a gypsy in Europe with Watson. She acknowledges her desire for her mother's acceptance: "I don't think she's ever forgiven me for running away with Watson" (75). Her journal records a longing for reconciliation: "if only I could speak to her" (114). Charleen's confessional self-transformation involves a renewal of the mother-daughter bond. Against a backdrop of concern about her mother's recent mastectomy, Charleen worries about her mother's loneliness and pending remarriage. She is especially concerned about her mother's silence: "She never told me she was even having an operation" (71). Florence McNinn is likewise defined by a lack that is partly linguistic. Charleen reflects on her mother's guidance and limited vocabulary that consists mainly of proverbs and clichés. More importantly, her mother is defined by a lack of authority that is associated with her gendered and ethnic identities: "I remind myself, above all, that she is weak" (122). Born of an illiterate mother who was an immigrant and peasant, Florence made the class jump to become a middle-class homemaker. Even her interior decorating is described as "an obsession ... to fill a terrible hurting void" (48). Charleen recognizes that her mother has received little compensation for her diligence. She also recognizes her own interconnection with her mother: "I am Florence McNinn's daughter, the genes are there, nothing I've done has scratched them out" (125). She identifies with her feminine lack and middle-class respectability: the "McNinn syndrome, [which] has riddled me with cowardice" (126). At the same time, she identifies with her mother's position as a survivor.

In her journal, Charleen explores her estrangement from the dominant discourses of individualism and autonomy. Like other feminist writers and critics, she attends to the mother-daughter relationship. By the end Charleen recognizes herself and her mother as survivors and provisional selves, perceptions that are embraced in a gendered confession. Charleen appreciates her mother's gesture in a crisis when she makes sandwiches while waiting for news of Seth's whereabouts. She thinks that it is a "kinship suddenly made substantial" (174). From interconnection springs confidence in oneself and others: "It was a night like this when Seth was born ... I had become serenely confident" (183). Upon remarrying, Florence takes a new name meaning cradle, Mrs Berceau, and Charleen sees the possibility of forming new identities for her mother and herself: "two is better than one" (210). This self-revelation enables Charleen to declare her love for Eugene. As the return home demonstrates, her childhood is over; and the journal ends with Charleen's embracing not a metaphysics of presence but a "metaphysic of survival" (213). This view represents both a feminine perspective and a feminist critique of individualism.

In addition to being presented as an interconnected self, Charleen is shown to be a discursive self. While she is no longer a child, she takes the opposite view of Watson. In a search for Seth that leads to Watson's apartment, she finds that her ex-husband resembles a baby because of his self-centredness. She discovers Watson in a mirror-enclosed room, which is carpeted with grass in box gardens and where he sits in a lotus position. He is an allegorical and parodic figure of masculine selfhood: "Adam, king of his rooming-house Eden" (188). Unlike Florence, Watson only blinks vacantly for a missing son: "to relieve suffering was an abstraction for him" (189). For Charleen the real is that which hurts. She is disillusioned again with Watson and the self that he represents. Posing as Brother Adam, a mentor and correspondent, he represents "an Emersonian vision of oneness ... a non-human form, a blind and speechless deity" (201). The self that is constituted in his letters is both discursive and reductive. His story becomes a structural metaphor or mise en abyme of the autobiographical space: "It was the mirrors, of course, huge mirrors mounted on two facing walls and lining the sloping ceiling, so that the small space seemed endless and unbelievably complex, like the sudden special openings that sometimes occur in dreams" (186–7). By analogy, the discursive self is necessarily specular, and autobiography is the mirror that "provokes fantasies of the real" (Gilmore, *Autobiographics* 16, 76). Unable to sustain this fiction of an identity, Watson goes to India in self-exile, just as he once fled his marriage.

In contrast to Brother Adam, who is no priest, Louis Berceau is a former priest. His name means cradle but he is no baby. He marries Charleen's mother and enters a new communal life with her family. Upon meeting Judith and Charleen, he takes each one to lunch at the Wayfarers' Inn, where Charleen confides in him as though he were a father or fellow pilgrim on the journey of life. Whereas Brother Adam is an ineffective interlocutor, Louis engages her and becomes an excellent listener. Charleen gives him an almost Shakespearean, seven-ages-of-man speech about Watson's multiple selves or incarnations, which range from the good son to the "piped and bearded" academic; she concludes that he is "a man without a centre" (154). She admits that she still wears his ring and that waiting for Watson is almost a daily religion. Louis accompanies her to the commune where Watson's absence provokes a transformative self-perception: "I will never again receive a message from Watson. Watson my lapsed-bastard, first-love, phantom husband. The last link ... has just been taken away from me" (165). This revelation distances Charleen from Watson, even as a Christlike Louis wipes away her tears.

Attention to the interlocutor characterizes Charleen's narrative as confessional and underscores the double figure of the confessor, a position that can be occupied by both speaker and listener. Charleen later meets readers of her poetry at Watson's former commune. Their assurance that they own her books and appreciate her work establishes her authority and opens up dialogue. The embedded encounters – with her readers, lovers, stepfather, mother, and sister – emphasize the "intersubjective exchange" that is a potential effect of confessional and autobiographical discourses (Smith and Watson 13–14). Encouraged by her readers, Charleen gives her books to her mother as a wedding gift. This act of good faith signals a self-transformation, but its provisional status is signalled by the recognition that life is fleeting: it is "perishable, vulnerable, and worthy" (208). Her confession is shaped by Judith's conviction that there is no "such thing as an ordinary person" (109), underlining the efficacy of the sisters' interaction.

In *The Box Garden*, Charleen's self-narration resembles life writing by other women in the 1970s. Gilmore remarks that similar auto-biographical writing is "framed within increasingly sophisticated critical discourses on the shifting displacements of 'identity' within language itself and on the possibility of political opposition based on testimonial and confessional writing as forms of resistance" (*Autobiographics* 41). The theorist points out that if "autobiography provokes fantasies of the real," a resistant reading of the autobiographical pact must explore "the constrained 'real' for the reworking of identity in the discourses of women's self-representation" (*Autobiographics* 239). Despite the novel's linearity of plot, the confessional search for self-transformation is interrupted and resisted by parodic and self-reflexive narrative strategies. In a series of confessions to Eugene, Judith, and Louis, and in an embedded search for the absent Watson, Charleen's journal is presented not as an embodiment of a metaphysics of presence, but as a metaphysics of survival. The effect is political in the simultaneous valorization of women's autobiographical production and inscription of a feminist critique of masculine figures of selfhood.

Although many critics view Shields's early novels as fictional autobiographies, they are not strictly autobiographical because they do not span a life from birth to death; rather, they present a slice of a life.[9] The term "fictional autobiography" is nonetheless helpful to locate Shields's work in a growing tradition of women's life writing. One must situate her in this tradition in order to historicize her work, instead of dismissing her novels as "women's books" in the way that Shields thought her critics did (Shields, qtd. in Wachtel, "Interview" 32). Before a feminist model emerged in Sylvia Plath's novel *The Bell Jar* (1963) – and before the Women's Movement of the 1970s, the period in which Shields was writing – the personal voice was used and developed by Jane Austen and Charlotte Brontë; nevertheless, as a literary practice it was dominated by men, ranging from Charles Dickens to J.D. Salinger (Lanser 189). Shields's awareness of literary history accounts for the irony that marks her fiction so clearly and consistently throughout her career. A historical grounding also accounts for her critical interest in autobiographical discourses, an interest that is evident in her early novels. She sees women's writing as undervalued but she argues, "I have never for one minute regarded the lives of women as trivial" (Shields, qtd. in De Roo 47). Susan Lanser insists upon reading the feminine narrative voice as an "intersection of social identity and textual form" – and a "critical locus of ideology" (15). If this reading is correct Linda Hutcheon rightly considers Shields a "postmodern artist" whose irony takes sexism as its target and who mounts a feminist challenge to established literary forms ("Power" 41).[10] This challenge takes the form of an embedded feminist critique of the dominant discourses of autobiography and literary criticism.

One of the possibilities of women's self-representation, which is evident but often ignored in Shields's early novels, is that, when read together, *Small Ceremonies* and *The Box Garden* demonstrate an experiment with multiple perspectives and the communal voice. In an interview with the *West Coast Review*, Shields herself admits that the two novels meet in "the sisters' different ways of looking at their childhood and their mother" (Shields, qtd. in De Roo 45). She mentions other intertexts including literary biography in *Small Ceremonies* and modern poetry in *The Box Garden*. She hints at a "structural secret" in *The Box Garden* (Shields, qtd in De Roo 47), by which she refers to another set of literary sisters: Susanna Moodie and Catharine Parr Traill, the elder and "more beautiful" of the two (Shields, qtd. in Wachtel, "Interview" 26). In her criticism of Moodie, Shields characterizes her work as demonstrating an autobiographical impulse (*Moodie* 13) and a tendency towards self-contradiction ("Afterword" 339), much like Judith's or Charleen's. Shields detects in Moodie a productive tension between the romantic and the realistic – fiction and non-fiction – as well as an embedded "strategy of survival" ("Afterword" 340). In *The Box Garden* there are echoes of still more literary sisters, when Charleen alludes to *Sense and Sensibility* in stating that "had we been shaped by a tradition of kindness and had our sensibility been monitored by learning, we might even have resembled Jane Austen's loving ... sisters" (123–4). Shields pays homage to Austen in that Judith represents sense, and Charleen represents sensibility. But both sisters display both traits at times, just as they do in Austen.[11] The communal voice is defined by Lanser as sequential, first-person "narration in which each voice speaks in turn," creating "collaborating 'I's'" (256). Shields's readers encounter "collaborating 'I's'" in her early novels. Here and throughout her work multiple stories contribute to "a fuller portrait" of women's communities; at the same time, there is an attempt to balance the tension between universality and difference.[12] While the communal voice risks erasing differences, the narratives in *Small Ceremonies* and *The Box Garden* are distinct enough to constitute a prime example of double-voicedness and multiple perspectives.

A historical view of Shields's early novels places them firmly in a growing tradition of women's life writing. It is an evolving tradition that encompasses more than autobiography, confession, and journal writing. Its social and political purpose is to reclaim the agency of the writing "self" even as it challenges literary genres. Her concept of life writing corresponds with Leigh Gilmore's understanding of contemporary women's autobiography: "Interruption is a discursive effect of gender politics and self-representation and evidences the possibilities and limitations on women's self-representation" (*Autobiographics* 49). Along with Gilmore, we must understand autobiography as a discursive hybrid that is not distinct from fiction but rather "aligned with fiction" (25). Gilmore reads in the discourses of truth and identity "those textual places where women's self-representation interrupts (or is interrupted by) the regulatory laws of gender and genre" (45). In Shields we find this type of resistant reading of the autobiographical pact. By using autobiographical modes in the contexts of crisis and metafiction, particularly the mise en abyme, Shields reproduces and at the same time subverts generic biases towards a subject that is masculine, singular, and autonomous. In gendered confessions that are self-reflexive, she reinscribes subjects that are feminine, multiple, and interconnected. Her subjects model not static, but dynamic selves that change in response to history and others. With the deliberate coupling of subjectivity and agency in her characters' self-writing, Shields lays the foundation of a feminist critique that she continues to develop throughout her writing career.

Chapter Two

The Problem of the Author: Absence and the Epitaph of Victim in *Swann*

Among the manuscripts of *Swann* in the Carol Shields archive lies a file folder marked "Swann pennies and dish 'belonging to Mary Swann.'" Opening the folder reveals two nesting envelopes. On the inner envelope appears a mysterious handwritten note: "Pennies found in a dish in Mary Swann's kitchen cupboard. The dish was a gift from Rose Hindmarch" (LMS-0212 1994–13 33).[1] Concealed in this envelope is an aluminum dish about the size of a soap dish and marked "Lake Champlain Ferries" along with several pennies. The dish was in all likelihood a souvenir from a reader, Edward Phillips, whose name appears on the outer envelope. Inside of it there is a business card with a note, dated February 1988 and addressed to Carol, about how much he had enjoyed the novel and not wanted it to end. If only for a moment, these notes cast doubt on the novel's status as fiction. Without further evidence of Swann's existence, and from the double quotation marks that set off the words "belonging to Mary Swann," one must conclude that the archive, like the novel, displays a self-conscious irony at work on the part of Shields and a deliberate desire to blur the line between fiction and reality.[2]

In the novel's embedded stories, similar to the nesting envelopes, Shields plays a game with the reader in order to question the boundary between fiction and non-fiction, especially in the life of Swann. The distinguishing feature of both biography and fictional biography is that they tell a life story; the same can be said of autobiography and fictional autobiography. Comparing fictional and historical life stories, narrative theorist Dorrit Cohn concludes that they all "tell the life of an *imaginary* person" (32; original emphasis). In other words, the art of character development is just as essential to life writing as it is to fiction. Cohn states that "the telling of lives" is "the generic region where factual and fictional narratives come into closest proximity, the territory that presents the greatest potential for overlap" (18). Shields is equally conscious of the arbitrary distinctions that critics make among genres – and the reader becomes increasingly aware of them while reading the life of Swann. Boundaries between fiction and non-fiction are crossed so often in *Swann* that the novel reads as a parody of biographical and autobiographical modes. At the same time, Shields's narrative insists upon its fictionality and frustrates attempts to draw direct correspondences between real and imaginary personages. In her portrait of the woman poet, Shields exploits for a political purpose the realist novel's convention of the typicality of character; and she does so in ways that recall the literary biography. By the novel's end, Shields's concern is evidently not only for the individual subject of Mary Swann, but also for the collective and gendered subject of women writers.

Cohn observes that non-fiction or history, of which autobiography and biography are subcategories, is more concerned with "humanity in the plural" than in the singular, which is the domain of realist novels that focus on a single life (18). Conversely, Cohn notes that "a novel that remained from start to finish in the mode of external focalization on its protagonist would strike us as something of an anomaly" (26). As a case in point, the narrative of *Swann* never depicts the thoughts of the poet who is the subject of its mock-biographical presentation. Creating an anomaly appears to be the purpose of ironically presenting embedded and multiple-voiced narratives about Swann. In effect, the more we hear about her, the less we know about her life and work. Eventually a portrait emerges, not of Swann, but of the literary community that mediates her reception as an author. The necessary slippage between fact and fiction, biography and novel, real and imaginary, is the all-too-real mystery that Shields explores, not the "whodunit" of a crime story. After all, the reader knows from the outset who killed Swann.

In fact, the novel is subtitled "A Mystery," a generic marker that appears in British but not American editions of *Swann*. Added by her publisher, Stoddart (Shields, qtd. in De Roo 50), the subtitle encourages our expectations of crime fiction in the subsequent narrative, though generic ambiguity abounds throughout the text. Cohn's comment about subtitles applies to *Swann*: "this overt frame is surrounded by another *covert* frame," which when discovered, would transform the narrative (Cohn 93; original emphasis). In this case, the novel would become a subversive and covert biography of a slain Canadian poet, Pat Lowther, whose life and death resemble Swann's and whose biography was unwritten at the time of the novel's publication. The narrative's genre is the greatest mystery of *Swann*, for it escapes categories (Roberts 124). Most importantly, it moves towards a pastiche of biography.[3]

Shields's novel explores, then, a generic problem and a social one. If we understand the work as life writing, as opposed to fiction, biography, or autobiography, we must consider it representative of a creative and critical practice. This idea is particularly useful in re-evaluating women's writing, because it signals a feminist challenge to literary boundaries that separate fiction and non-fiction; and life writing offers a way of rereading literary canons that undervalue women writers (Kadar, *Essays* 3–4, 10). This is the point of Shields's narrative about Swann – and by extension, perhaps Lowther – as an erased and absent author. Life writing permits Shields to experiment with self-reflexive and metafictional narratives as well as non-linear or fragmented ones. By mixing genres and categories – which include genre and gender categories – women have successfully challenged established canons. Shields effectively makes this point not only in her novel, but also in her criticism of writers such as Susanna Moodie.

Furthermore, women's life writing permits a critical re-examination of everyday life and ordinary people, as opposed to great people, especially men who write autobiographical and historical works. In her preface to the Random House edition of *Swann* (1995), Shields poses an important question that is central to the novel: "What transformative power allows an ordinary person like Mary Swann to achieve extraordinary results, and can we ever really know that person?" In her novel Shields interrogates further the relationship between text and author, just as Michel Foucault does in his essay "What Is an Author?" He argues that although the text appears to point to a figure who is outside the text and who precedes it, the "mark of the writer is reduced to nothing more than the singularity of his absence; he must assume the role of the dead man in the game of writing" (198). As a murdered woman, Mary Swann is, in the words of her discoverer, "dead. Exceedingly dead" (6). However, her literary reputation is in the process of being constructed, appropriated, circulated, and valorized; in other words, the name

"Mary Swann" is being transformed into what Foucault would call the "author-function" ("Author" 202). Her reputation remains in question. Thus, Shields parodies the literary process of author-construction in the case of Swann, a fictional and representative woman writer; moreover, it is a social process with real material effects in the probable model and only-alluded-to life of Lowther. In the form of a feminist critique, the narrative satirizes the mediators of cultural production, including Swann's publisher, critic, biographer, librarian, and bookseller.

While critics have noted the parody of the author-construction in *Swann*,[4] the novel also creates another level of parody that deliberately crosses boundaries between fiction and non-fiction. This parody draws the reader's attention to social inequalities on the basis of gender in cases of female authorship. In its evocation of a real author, this parody recalls the theoretical manoeuvres and cultural critique of Shields's first novel and its references to Moodie. *Swann* similarly alludes to the real author Pat Lowther in its descriptions of the fictional Mary Swann. The murdered Swann is romanticized as a tragic figure, just as the murdered Lowther is romanticized to the detriment of the reception of her work. The work of both women is largely forgotten. In a masked and oblique engagement with a real life, Shields's text reads against the grain of a Foucauldian discourse of the author-function – insofar as it posits the disappearance of a *male* author – in a feminist critique of dominant representations and de facto erasures of women writers. Shields's critique is significant precisely because a woman's work cannot be accepted as literary until endowed with the author-function.

The woman who serves as a model for Swann is in reality considered exemplary; in fact, an annual award for Canada's best female poet is named after her. That is not to say Lowther is necessarily *the* template, but rather a probable template for Swann. Like Swann, Lowther was impoverished in life and bludgeoned to death by a domineering husband. Both writers are posthumously published and publicly eulogized. Wendy Roy notes the resemblance of these life stories ("Autobiography" 140), as does Margaret Atwood in "To the Light House," a tribute to Carol Shields in the *Guardian* after Shields died of complications from breast cancer in 2003. Shields denied making any conscious reference to Lowther in *Swann*. However, as Lowther's most recent biographer, Christine Wiesenthal, points out, the reputations of Swann and Lowther are similarly constructed (301–2), appropriated, and circulated under the epitaph of *victim* (85). Whether or not Lowther is a conscious model for Swann, Shields evokes the memory of Lowther as representative of a cultural politics that romanticizes women writers, even as the novelist parodies the author-construction. We can be certain that Shields was aware of Lowther, for she was an enthusiastic listener at a poetry reading by Lowther in 1974 at the University of Ottawa (Wiesenthal 82). Shields and Lowther published poetry with the same literary press in Ottawa called Borealis; they were reviewed together by *Saturday Night*'s Robert Fulford; and they were both identified by literary critic George Woodcock as promising Canadian writers in 1975 (Wiesenthal 110). In her fiction Shields exaggerates the very real image of the woman as a victim, in order to show how this image limits Swann's reception and relegates her to the rank of a minor poet. In her resistance to this gender stereotype, Shields reaffirms the value of women's writing as an important, though neglected, contribution to literary history.

The lives and deaths of Swann and Lowther share many details in the process of author-construction. Swann is described as poor, a fact repeated like a refrain, because it recalls a romantic myth of the poet as a solitary genius, while reiterating a disavowal of the economic and material processes of literary production (Bourdieu 79). Swann has little education and a rural, working-class background. A farm wife on unproductive land, she never has "two nickels to rub together."[5] She lacks clothes for church and wears to her publisher's house "a shapeless black coat, hideous thick fawn stockings and rubber overshoes" (265). She has no briefcase to carry her poems, only a paper bag. The publisher claims that she has an ordinary face except for two missing teeth. She has no driver's licence, dental records, or medical records. She possesses only a library card. Like Swann's life, Lowther's is often described as one of poverty. She was raised in North Vancouver and left school at the age of sixteen. Lowther attended readings of the Vancouver Poetry Society in the late 1950s and 1960s, appearing with a lean face but "nicely dressed" (Grescoe 17). She and her husband, who was also a working-class poet, sometimes lived on social assistance (Brooks 101). In a CBC radio documentary and posthumous tribute, host Peter Gzowski called Lowther "penniless," while publisher Allan Safarik said that he had once asked her, "For God's sake, why don't you get your teeth fixed?" She replied, "I can't afford to." Poet Marya Fiamengo called

Lowther's teeth "a metaphor for her life" because of their obvious neglect. Modest grants from the Canada Council for the Arts were deducted from the Lowthers' welfare cheques or spent on groceries and dental care for their children; nevertheless, the grants symbolized a degree of "literary validation" (Wiesenthal 170). Only one month before her death, Lowther was on salary for teaching creative writing at the University of British Columbia. Lowther's life clearly demonstrates "class tensions between various fields of literary production" (Wiesenthal 114). At the same time, it reveals the disadvantages associated with her class and gender.

In death, Swann and Lowther share the epitaph of *victim*. Both are killed by their husbands, and their works are overshadowed by their violent deaths. Swann's husband shoots her in the head, hits her face with a hammer, dismembers her body, and hides it in a silo. The body is found one week later when her husband commits suicide. She is only fifty years old. Similarly, Lowther's husband attacked his forty-year-old wife with a hammer, fractured her skull, put her body in the trunk of a car, and dropped it from a cliff at Furry Creek near Squamish between 23 and 25 September 1975. On 13 October 1975 her naked body was discovered and later identified by dental records. Roy Lowther was convicted of murder and sentenced to life imprisonment on 23 April 1977. The lives and deaths of Swann and Lowther are uncannily parallel and separated by only a decade. Swann lived from 1915 to 1965; Lowther, from 1935 to 1975. Most importantly to readers of the novel, both are remembered as victims. Swann is dubbed "*that poor woman, her head cut off even*" (48; original emphasis), and the critic who discovers her thinks, "This woman was a total victim" (317). Sadly, her work is eclipsed by the sensationalized stories of her death.

Similarly, the reputation of Lowther is "buried under the epitaph of 'victim'" (Wiesenthal 112). In a corrective reading that focuses critical attention on the poet's life and work, Wiesenthal asserts, "Lowther has been artfully rewritten and artlessly forgotten" (118). For example, Paul Grescoe's "Eulogy for a Poet" ran in a national newspaper insert in 1976, with a photo caption that read, "The Poet as Victim: Pat Lowther," and a subtitle that declared "Pat Lowther lived passively, wrote lyrically and died violently." Grescoe attributes the word "passive" to Lowther's friend, Lorraine Vernon, who described her as a "victim" who was "beautiful but passive" (Grescoe 19). Wiesenthal gives the comment some context: Vernon had helped her houseclean before Lowther's "aborted attempt" to leave Roy while he was on a canoe trip in 1973 (183). Her publishers, Patrick Lane and Seymour Mayne, claimed that friends had even offered a truck to help her move (Lane 30; Brooks 94). In 1975, Lowther still planned to leave when her children were older because she could not raise them alone and find the time to write (Brooks 104). Though some called her "passive" in life, Lowther's poetic voice is not at all passive. Woodcock calls it "austere" in the CBC documentary. Atwood states in a letter to *Ms.* magazine, "I didn't think she was that passive" (qtd. in Brooks 143). Clearly, not everyone sees her as a victim.

Shortly after her death in 1975, media tributes continued to represent Lowther as a victim and perhaps a prophetess. The CBC documentary emphasizes her gender in its title "Pat Lowther: Woman, Mother, Artist," even as it depicts Lowther as an unsung hero and poet with a "premonition of her own death." Cited as examples of prescience on the radio, and later in print by Fulford, are poems such as "Kitchen Murder," "To a Woman Who Died of 34 Stab Wounds," and "City Slide / 6" in which these lines appear: "Love is an intersection / where I have chosen / unwittingly to die" (234; Fulford 71). Lowther's death was certainly tragic, for she had just been appointed as a university lecturer and chair of the League of Canadian Poets. But in the documentary poet Dorothy Livesay repeated the romantic myth: "The stars were not kind to Pat." Also in the documentary, poet Milton Acorn anticipated Lowther's reputation as Canada's Sylvia Plath, though he believed she was "no Sylvia Plath" because she "had no hand in her own destiny." He points to an ideological fascination with violence and death in dominant discourses about women. Critics continue to read into Lowther's poems a hyperreal[6] or self-fulfilling prophecy of her death. In contrast, Shields's narrative compares Swann to Plath, only to raise an ethical question about the practice of literary biography. Morton Jimroy, Swann's biographer, is asked about his responsibility to the subject: "What if the body of work is still alive and breathing? ... Take Sylvia Plath – " (96). Shields evokes critical controversies that surround women writers in order to subvert reductive readings of their literary legacies. As Wiesenthal remarks, the "claims about Pat Lowther have tended ... to replicate polarized extremes of critical over- and under-valuation" (37). A similar polarization of opinions occurs with Swann.

Readings of Swann's work as strangely prophetic reinforce the romantic stereotype of the poet as a seer. In the Swann Memorial Room at a museum in Nadeau, Ontario, a didactic panel highlights "the prophetic poem entitled 'The Silo.'" A curator and librarian, Rose Hindmarch selects materials to suggest that Swann had an uncanny sense of her own impending death "seven years before the poet's untimely demise" (159). This representation is neither logically nor ethically sound, and Shields's exaggeration exposes the post hoc fallacy. At the same time, her irony underscores a theoretical and critical issue: the absence of the author. This absence is evocative of the romantic myth of the poet, which Foucault identifies as part of a literary historical tradition that extends to the present from the Greek epic, particularly its elevation of the author to a type of immortality:

> Our culture has metamorphosed this idea of narrative, or writing, as something designed to ward off death. Writing has become linked to sacrifice ... it is now a voluntary effacement which does not need to be represented in books, since it is brought about in the writer's very existence. The work, which once had the duty of providing immortality, now possesses the right to kill, to be its author's murderer. ("Author" 198)

Consequently, the writer is reduced to a trace in the text. Shields represents Swann's absence through the construction and appropriation of the author-function by not only her curator, but her publisher, critic, and biographer. Rose Hindmarch, Frederic Cruzzi, Sarah Maloney, and Morton Jimroy, respectively, all engage in author-construction for their own peculiar ends. These characters are the mediators of cultural production who consecrate and sustain the meaning and value of a literary work, although their engagement with the author is suspect.

Foucault identifies four traits of the author-function that, in the context of *Swann*, may be called attribution, appropriation, circulation, and valorization ("Author" 202–5). Shields's narrative addresses the trait of attribution – that is, the author-construction. Just as Swann's reputation rests upon a posthumous collection, *Swann's Songs*, Lowther's reputation relies on a posthumously published work, *A Stone Diary* (Oxford, 1977). In fact, there has been some speculation that the title of Lowther's last work inspired the title of Shields's novel *The Stone Diaries*. More problematic than the posthumous collection are the only somewhat reliable *Time Capsule* (Polestar, 1996) and unreliable *Final Instructions* (West Coast Review/Orca Sound, 1980). The former was compiled with the assistance of Lowther's daughters who served as her literary executors; and the latter, with her former lover who supposedly provided from memory twenty-five previously unpublished poems. Neither this man, Ward Carson, nor the editor of *Final Instructions*, a journalist named Dona Sturmanis, can point to an original manuscript (Wiesenthal 102). In this way, they are like Swann's editors, Frederic and Hildë Cruzzi. Unlike Swann, however, Lowther produced three additional volumes of poetry during her lifetime: *This Difficult Flowring* ([sic], Very Stone House, 1968), *The Age of the Bird* (Blackfish Press, 1972), and *Milk Stone* (Borealis, 1974). All were published by small presses, just as *Swann's Songs* is published by Peregrine Press, the home operation of a journalist from Kingston, Ontario.

Frederic Cruzzi, the publisher of *Swann's Songs*, begins the process of author-construction with a printrun of only two hundred fifty copies. He later regards the clichéd title as a lapse of judgment, but he continues to promote the poet as a "glorious, gifted crone" (275). Because he published her early poems in the newspaper of which he is the editor and publisher, Swann offers him one hundred twenty-five poems, which he considers to be original. The poems suit his wife and co-editor's policy to seek new talent: "New sounds ... and innovative technique, but work that turns on a solid core of language" (256). Hildë Cruzzi also engages in author-construction to an unusual degree with her editorial interventions. Half of the small pieces of paper on which Swann's poems are written are inadvertently damaged, when the publisher's wife uses the paper bag that contains them to dispose of fish bones. Because Swann wrote her poems with a fountain pen, the ink runs on the wet paper and becomes almost illegible. An aspiring poet herself, Hildë Cruzzi attempts to reconstruct the poems. She and her husband have "puzzled and conferred over every blot, then guessed, then invented" what they name "the manuscript" (281). The Cruzzis justify their reconstruction of Swann by arguing that "they owed Mrs Swann an interpretation that would reinforce her strengths as a poet" (282). Shields parodies the absence of the author by emphasizing that Hildë Cruzzi almost "seemed to be inhabiting, she said, another woman's body" (281). In the end there is no surviving manuscript of Swann's work, just as there is none for Lowther's projected work, *Final Instructions.*

This scene perhaps alludes to Lowther's poem "Kitchen Murder." The description of the Cruzzis' kitchen with its "electrical appliances, a blender, a toaster" may appear to be banal; however, the kitchen is a site of both domestic life and domestic violence (286). Frederic Cruzzi knocks his wife to the floor upon discovering the damaged poems. That same evening Swann's husband kills his wife in her own kitchen. Lowther's poem creates irony by suggesting that ordinary kitchenware, such as "the automatic perc," meat forks, and plates, may be used in a fight: "Everything here's a weapon" (237). It is likely that Shields alludes to "Kitchen Murder" because it is so often quoted in reference to Lowther's death – in Grescoe's eulogy, Gzowski's tribute, and Fulford's review of *A Stone Diary* – as evidence that "death haunts [her] poems" (Fulford 71). Shields's narrative demonstrates that the tragic deaths of women writers are sometimes read into their work as inviting death. Such readings are reductive and a form of scapegoating that can perpetuate a cultural fiction of women's willingness to become victims. It is ironic that Swann died and wrote her poetry in the kitchen, a room where Lowther also worked (Wiesenthal 174), just as Shields herself did. A further irony is implied by the murderer's motive: envy of her literary success.

The kitchens of the Cruzzis and the Swanns are domestic and social spaces in which women's work is writing and not just cooking. Kitchens and texts are also sites of struggle. The risk of violence or exclusion demonstrates the all-too-real dangers of women's silencing, as Lowther's life shows. Her first book, *This Difficult Flowring,* explores domestic themes such as sexuality, marriage, and motherhood, suggesting her active "participation in the larger project of Canadian women's writing" in the 1960s and 1970s (Wiesenthal 164). In Lowther, domesticity signals a feminine perspective and an "effort to *make space* in the literary public domain for women's private ... experience" (Wiesenthal 166; original emphasis). The same might be said of Shields. To say that Shields's work reacts against feminism rather than participates in it is inaccurate. But in "Still in the Kitchen: The Art of Carol Shields," Laura Groening makes this very claim. She falsely accuses Shields of a lack of political will: "The women's movement is mocked ... in each of Shields' novels" (16). Groening focuses not on Swann, but on Maloney as a feminist who is "in love with good clothes and her self-image" and who "becomes pregnant ... and immediately rejects her earlier political commitment" (17). It is true that in Shields's fiction no critic is beyond reproach, but Groening oversimplifies Shields's purpose and narrative intent: "What Shields' novels do best is to capture the daily reality of the ordinary middle-class (often academic) family" (14). She insists that Shields leaves women in the kitchen and uses domestic spaces as transparent and untroubled representations of "domestic contentment" (16). Groening assumes from the words the implied author puts in the mouths of her characters that the real author takes an anti-feminist stance. Strangely, this argument is another form of murdering the author.

In fact, Shields gives the representation of domestic space an ironic twist, as demonstrated by the violent scenes in the kitchens of the Cruzzis and the Swanns. Linda Hutcheon rightly remarks that "the feminist challenges of artists like ... Carol Shields" are "articulated in the form of irony" ("Power" 41). She does not find Shields guilty by association with domesticity; rather, she sees Shields's irony as self-conscious and "used to create an 'insider' position from which to enable a critique from within" dominant discourses (Hutcheon, "Power" 37). Hutcheon concedes that irony's "power of contesting is limited" because postmodernism is "not the radical, utopian oppositionality of the modernist avant-garde"; but irony is not necessarily "politically quietistic" (45). By the means of irony and parody Shields's text demonstrates its political purpose. Its irony and historical allusions can inform our understanding of Shields's feminist critique of Swann's – and Lowther's – reception.

Like Swann's publishers, Lowther's engage in author-construction, attributing to Lowther works that are original but neglected. Patrick Lane, the publisher of her first book, perceives her as an "outsider" to the literary institution even though he regards her as "the finest woman poet in the country" (Lane, qtd. in Finlay 16). Another publisher, Allan Safarik, says, "She didn't get half the acclaim she deserved." He reinforces the victim stereotype by romanticizing her death as ill-fated: "She was star-crossed" (Safarik, qtd. in Finlay 16). But a romantic discourse obscures a literary politics that is also influenced by nationalism. Cruzzi suggests as much when he laments that another poet is too good for a Canadian audience, because the lines are unrhymed and celebrate more than the Canadian landscape. The work is deemed too international but Cruzzi values it because he was born in France to a Muslim father. Swann's verse rhymes and it is relatively original; nevertheless, as a woman unconnected to a literary community, she remains a minor poet.

After exposing the problem of attribution, Shields's narrative addresses the appropriation of the author as a trait of the author-function. Despite Swann's initial neglect by literary critics, her poetry is discovered after death by an American feminist. Maloney reclaims Swann as a woman writer who has played a role in reinventing modern poetry; Maloney herself plays the role of Swann's "literary executor" (32). Having found Swann's book at a cabin while on vacation, Maloney writes the first critical article on Swann's work and continues the process of author-construction. She argues that Swann is an original and "self-generated" artist (339), as well as a female "model of endurance and survival" (55). However, she scorns Jimroy's romantic attempts to canonize Swann as a solitary genius: he lauds her work as a "miniaturized, spontaneous, virgin birth" (338). In the same way, Lowther's "metaphorical canonization has in effect pre-empted her availability for critique" (Wiesenthal 111). Jimroy's author-construction reproduces a modernist myth of the artist as a lone hero. Instead, the artist works within a network of social agents and cultural mediators in the field of literary production (Bourdieu 46). The canonization of some authors in literary discourse, to the exclusion of others, imitates religious discourse with its "dialect of orthodoxy" (Bourdieu 34), while effecting political struggles that are ongoing within a wider "field of power" (37). That wider field includes gender relations.

Shields both reproduces and exposes power relations among cultural mediators by using personal names for feminine characters, such as Sarah and Rose, and family names for masculine characters, such as Jimroy and Cruzzi. The surname or "patronym represents public identity," while the personal name represents private identity (Gilmore, *Autobiographics* 88), signalling a cultural politics that divides the sexes into separate spheres. By exaggerating a lack of parallelism in the use of men's and women's names, Shields exposes an ideological gap and parodies hierarchical relations based on gender: "Such binary distinctions are definitional strategies, part of the production and maintenance of the technologies of truth and linked to their hierarchizing organizations of knowledge" and bodies (*Autobiographics* 88). By heightening a binary opposition of personal and family names, Shields's parody sets a trap, into which critics fall when they call only female characters by their personal names. Thus, Shields's ironic twist deliberately puts a "torque on ordinary discourse" ("Arriving" 250). Only partly aware of her power as a critic, Maloney catches herself comparing Swann's poetry to a rosary with "little wooden beads I can manipulate on a cord" (61). Although she mocks Jimroy, she participates as much as he does in a re-mystification of the author and the work. Her words evoke, to borrow Foucault's words, "the notion of writing [that] seems to transpose the empirical characteristics of the author into a transcendental anonymity" ("Author" 199). This consecration of the author by the process of author-construction is just as profitable to the critic as to the bookseller because it increases the monetary value of both the primary work and the secondary criticism. Because a primary work is accepted as literary only when it is endowed with the author-function (Foucault, "Author" 203), the game for Maloney becomes one of rediscovering the author. Shields's narrative underlines the process of appropriation.

Maloney thinks, "In a sense I invented Mary Swann and am responsible for her" (30). Despite her self-professed ethical responsibility, Maloney withholds Swann's notebook from others because it contains only weather notes and grocery lists – like the scraps of paper left in Lowther's archive (Wiesenthal 174) – and it does not constitute a literary work, as a journal or autobiography might. Maloney also disposes of the only other artefact, Swann's rhyming dictionary, because she fears it will support competing author-constructions of Swann as a *poète naïve*. By her words and actions, Maloney appropriates Swann to a feminist discourse as a literary foremother. Maloney valorizes her poetry for its "expression of female sensuality ... the clear contours of birth and regeneration" (56). As Mary Eagleton comments, "Swann will be constructed ... as a lost woman writer," even though the "*habitus* of Swann, shaped in social conditions of rural isolation, patriarchal and class oppression, mean poverty, and maternal expectations makes it surprising that she is able to act on even these limited possibilities" ("Reading " 317, 319). Maloney is personally and professionally invested in a feminist project of reclaiming Swann; her reputation as a critic depends on Swann's reception as a consecrated poet. She attributes to Swann the creative power of the author-function, and she becomes competitive and possessive: "Mary Swann's notebook is mine" (27). She is unconscious of what Foucault calls the "projection, in more or less psychologizing terms, of the operations that we force texts to undergo, the connections that we make, the traits that we establish as pertinent, the continuities that we recognize, or the exclusions that we practice" ("Author" 203). In addition to the feminist critic, many other critics are engaged in the same biographical enterprise at the Swann Symposium. As Brian Johnson points out, "*Swann* parodies and undercuts the pretensions of its critics, revealing an academic power-play that manifests itself at several textual levels in recurring acts of appropriation" (212). Once again, no critic is beyond reproach in Shields's fiction.

Shields observed firsthand the expansion of Canadian studies in universities across Canada during the late 1960s and early 1970s, particularly the inauguration of annual symposia on Canadian writers at the University of Ottawa, such as the Grove Symposium (Hammill, "Native" 89). There Shields did her graduate work in Canadian literature under the supervision of feminist critic Lorraine McMullen. An American-born writer who became a Canadian citizen only after marriage, Shields takes a wry view of Canadian nationalism.[7]

Swann's biographer, Jimroy, is as eager as Maloney to appropriate Swann and attribute to her the author-function. He is, after all, a modernist with a romantic impulse to search for "the key to Swann's genius" (136). In a lecture on biography he claims that "from common clay, works of genius evolve" (96), echoing Shields's prefatory remark in her novel about the ordinary person's potential to achieve extraordinary results if constructed as an author. Swann initially appeals to him as a biographical subject because she is an enigma. However, Jimroy becomes frustrated because her life resists the biographical form. He concludes that hers is "one of the dullest lives ever lived" (89), except for a violent and dramatic death. Like Maloney, he excludes information about the ordinariness of Swann's letters, especially one about buying underwear. He frets that the life and work do not match (132). The biographer's task is to establish that the author's discourse is "not ordinary everyday speech" but rather speech that "must receive a certain status" (Foucault, "Author" 201). He must also distinguish the author's name, or identity, from any other proper name. Without documentary evidence, he invents literary influences, choosing canonical writers such as Emily Dickinson and Jane Austen. At the same time, he suppresses the influence of popular writers such as Margaret Mitchell, Edna Ferber, and "Mother Goose" (111), who are suggested to him by Hindmarch and

Swann's daughter, Frances Moore. He wishes to avenge Swann's silencing by her husband and by critics who ignore her work, and he competes with Maloney, and with Willard Lang who makes similar claims about "Swann's unique genius" (338). Perhaps more than Maloney, Jimroy demonstrates the Foucauldian notion that writers' discourses are objects of appropriation ("Author" 202). He admits, "It was just a matter of time before the theoreticians got to Mary Swann and tore her limb from limb in a grotesque parody of her bodily death" (95). Still, he romanticizes Swann as "Mother Soul" (103) and promotes his biography for its mystique of elegy, recalling Paul Grescoe's biographical sketch of Lowther (97). Jimroy secretly fears he has silenced Swann by "shutting her up" in a "miniature act of murder" (134). He betrays an odd mixture of self-awareness and misogyny. He participates in a re-victimization of Swann by appropriating her to an outmoded modernist discourse; he even steals her fountain pen and one of two existing photos of her.

Shields's parodic portrait of the biographer echoes some real literary practices. Lowther's first biographer, Toby Brooks, resembles Jimroy in neither action nor intent, yet she resembles Maloney in her critical approach. As a second-wave feminist Brooks appropriates Lowther's life to a feminist discourse. She stresses themes of female sexuality and birth that coincide with the rise of the Women's Movement: "By 1975, people were saying that Pat was a feminist" (175). Brooks plays up Lowther's tragic death as an example of domestic violence, but she downplays the prosecution's case of poetry rivalry, which suggests a startling motive for murder. Roy Lowther envied his wife's invitation to read at a poetry evening sponsored by the New Democratic Party in the Vancouver Ironworkers' Hall, since he considered himself to be a working-man's poet (Wiesenthal 30). Lowther's murder demonstrates that deadly rivalries exist in the literary field, as Shields's narrative shows. Unlike Swann, however, Lowther did not write in isolation. She published her poetry. She gave readings with other West Coast poets, such as Lane, Safarik, and Mayne, and many of them were her friends, including Livesay and Vernon. She was elected by her peers as a chair of the League of Canadian Poets, an organization that later created the annual Pat Lowther Memorial Award for the best book of poems by a woman. In spite of the complex social contexts that shaped Lowther's life and work, Brooks repeats the romanticism of early tributes to Lowther: "Heaven had not dealt Pat the best hand at the card table" (115).

Brooks later coordinated a memorial reading for the twentieth anniversary of Lowther's death in an event called "The Triumph of Pat Lowther." While such action is laudable, the establishment of separate awards for women writers reinforces women's marginalization in the literary institution.[8]

Just as Jimroy and Maloney appropriate Swann to modernist and feminist discourses, Hindmarch appropriates her to realist and nationalist ones. Hindmarch perpetuates the poet's image as "a distinguished, though minor, contributor to the body of Canadian literature" (159). The librarian repeats the biographer's claim that Swann was Canada's Emily Dickinson. She participates in the Swann Symposium by providing photos, and she gives Maloney the notebook and the rhyming dictionary that the critic later discards. Hindmarch challenges Jimroy to return the photo that he stole from the museum in Nadeau, but she covets the fountain pen that Moore cherished and the love poems that Lang found in Swann's kitchen. She presents as historical artefacts many objects that are only "*similar* to those found in Mary Swann's rural home" (205; original emphasis). She buys them at antique shops and rummage sales and justifies what appears to be a lie: "The charm of falsehood is not that it distorts reality, but that it creates reality afresh" (205). She reconstructs Swann's life as lean and useful. She represents herself to others as a friend of Swann, but she admits the sin of deceit. She never spoke with Swann about her family or books. Perhaps out of guilt for Swann's lonely death, Hindmarch withholds the fact that a biographer would find most useful: she is the one who told Swann to show her poetry to a nearby publisher (207). Swann was not as isolated as Jimroy and Maloney think, and solidarity among women is potentially transformative. Jimroy seeks the "one central cathartic event" that a biography requires for character development (135). But Hindmarch keeps it a secret.

Like Hindmarch, acquaintances of Lowther attempt to purge a sense of guilt for her neglect or abuse. For example, Vernon admits to a survivor's guilt in a special section of *Contemporary Verse Two* in January of 1976: "My friend, how fitting / in death I should attend / to details of your Memorial" (Brewster et al. 17). She makes restitution by offering "lines" on the "altar of your honour." Elizabeth Brewster also confesses, "Forgive me, gentle ghost. / Haunt my mind's / passageways / with your grace" (16). The canonization that is implied by the word "grace" occurs again in P.K. Page's list of feminine virtues for Lowther, who is "observant, courteous, modest" and quiet but quick to care for others (Brewster et al. 16). For more than a decade after Lowther's death and until Shields's novel was published in 1988, writers such as Margaret Atwood, Seymour Mayne, and Daniel David Moses continued to romanticize Lowther's death in poems that are often anthologized. In "Another Night Visit" Atwood describes the uncanny return of the memory of Lowther:

> alive still, moving
> around each word like
> wind, these words un-
> earth you. (60)

In "For Pat Lowther (1935–1975)," Mayne calls her a sacrificial lamb: "Sheepishly you bruised / yourself against sharp / sticks and thorns" (118). Moses reveres Lowther as "Our Lady of the Glacier," whose "words / keep surfacing," only to "drop from our own lips like stones" (47). Representations of women as victims or scapegoats recur as cultural projections and gender stereotypes in the life story of Swann as well.

A more measured response to the return of a traumatic memory appears in Atwood's review of Lowther's *A Stone Diary*. Atwood states that "reviewing a dead poet pressures the reviewer into declaiming like Brutus over Caesar's corpse ... Tribute, we feel, must be paid ... The pull towards elegy is strong" ("Last" 307). She contradicts myths of female passivity and fascination with death: "Lowther was no more preoccupied with violence than are most serious poets of the twentieth century" (308). She reads in Lowther's work traces of an "integration of her socialist politics with a personal vision on one side and a biological and cosmological one on the other" (309). Again Atwood quips, "Women, incidentally, are sometimes classed with things, and therefore innocent" (312). Similarly to Atwood, Shields exposes stereotypes of women that appear in critics' characterization of Swann as passive.

Shields's text refers ironically to Swann's innocence. Because "the innocent need protection," Maloney becomes Swann's self-appointed "defender" (32). Jimroy thinks that Swann's originality comes "out of an innocent, ignorant groping in the dark" (96). He interviews Swann's daughter but she offers insufficient evidence to support his thesis. In a comparable role, Lowther's daughters played a part in preserving their mother's memory by contributing to the posthumously published *Time Capsule* (1996). In the collection's autobiographical and introductory essay, Beth Lowther offers a feminist view of her mother's victimhood in stating that her father was "deeply threatened by her [mother's] frank openness to sexuality" (18). The collection seeks to honour Lowther's memory but it falls somewhat short of its goal by offering no chronology or sources of previously unpublished poems. In the preface, editor Michelle Benjamin suggests that the new poems came from notebooks and "a manuscript that Lowther was working on at the time of her death" (15). Although Lowther once mentioned at a reading her plan for a book called *Time Capsule*, the file for the so-called manuscript contained only seven poems (Wiesenthal 106). *Time Capsule* contributes to the knowledge of Lowther's work but also shows her critical neglect, being for over a decade the only collection in print since *A Stone Diary* was remaindered in 1981. Only recently published is *The Collected Works of Pat Lowther* (NeWest 2010).

After exploring social processes of attribution and appropriation, Shields's narrative addresses the problems of circulation and distribution as part of the author-function. In *Swann*, the bookseller proves the most culpable of mediators by limiting circulation of the poet's work. Although the critics' actions reveal their political interestedness and "scholarly greed" (357), even they are surprised to discover Sam Brown's theft of almost all remaining copies of *Swann's Songs* in an attempt to drive up prices. He has stolen other artefacts such as the fountain pen and photos with the aid of Lang, the conference chair.[9] A literary murder of the author is committed by Brown when he throws Swann's papers out of a window, just as Roy Lowther once threw his wife's briefcase into the bushes at Furry Creek. As Buss contends, the novel reveals that "in the case of women subjects who often suffer from as great a repression of their production after death as in their lives, we must write 'beyond the epitaph' [of *victim*]" ("Abducting" 433; emphasis added). Shields's narrative shows that in the masculine-dominated field of literary production, political struggles over manuscripts, interpretations, and reputations are a significant but erased part of the biography of a woman writer.

In addition to attribution, appropriation, and circulation, Shields's narrative addresses valorization as the final trait that Foucault identifies as part of the author-function. He concedes, "The author-function does not affect all discourses in a universal and constant way." He finds instead that "in a civilization like our own there are a certain number of discourses that are endowed with the 'author-function,' while others are deprived of it" ("Author" 202). It is for this reason that Shields gives her narrative a feminist twist. The lives of women writers are further marginalized by their resistance to literary biography. Unlike Ezra Pound, Jimroy's initial biographical subject, Swann "did *not* write scholarly articles or essays elucidating her poetic theories" (340; original emphasis). Swann apparently disappoints Jimroy, because of what Maloney calls his "holy attitude toward prime materials" (56). In Lang's view, too, even the feminist critic who rediscovers Swann merits only a footnote. Swann's life reads like a "cautionary tale" (Barbour 255) about gender as a basis of exclusion in literary practices. In this respect, Swann's story once again recalls Lowther's.

Following Bourdieu, theorist Toril Moi reconceptualizes the literary field as contained within the broader field of power relations, and gender as a "social category" within that field (1019). When read from a critical perspective such as hers, the novel does not support Brian Johnson's conclusion that *Swann* demonstrates that "the author still functions" (228). He misinterprets the narrative as simply ironic when, in fact, Shields employs an ironic twist and a feminist twist in a feminist double strategy. He thinks that "*Swann* dramatizes the full progress of Foucault's argument, beginning with the Barthesian premise of the dead author and his subsequent re-examination of 'the privileges of the subject' ... through his notion of the author function as it guides and limits Sarah, Jimroy, and Rose's respective readings of the Swann poems" (212). While Johnson is correct in stating that Shields parodies the pretensions of the critics inside the text, her parody also extends outside the text to Foucault, especially with the final poem "Lost Things." Not all writers disappear into the text in the same manner or to the same degree. Swann's poem is reconstructed by scholars at the symposium when all of her papers and texts are actually lost, and yet the attribution of her poem remains in question at the end. If the woman writer is valorized at all, it is by Shields's narrative itself. In poetry and narrative alike, women writers use the autobiographical mode to claim and create spaces from which to speak, and their voices resonate. Shields's narrative thus functions in a more complex way than Johnson suggests. It becomes, in Gilmore's words, a "discourse of re-membering and self-restoration written against the language of privation" (*Autobiographics* 90).

Shields's text reads as a discursive and social practice of resistance by remembering and valorizing Swann.

In contrast to the academic piracy that ironizes and discredits the discursive practices of other characters, Shields's narrative never ironizes Swann's words. Instead, her work is taken seriously and her poetry is represented favourably as lyrical, economical, and unsentimental. Her lines deal poignantly with loss, and even though they rhyme, they are sophisticated (Clara Thomas, "Fragments" 203); moreover, they are sufficiently ambiguous to suggest a multiplicity of meanings. By such means as creating stylistic allusions and biographical similarities, Shields pays tribute to Lowther's work. Lowther's personal lyrics in *This Difficult Flowring* are in fact described by Hilda Thomas as "elegant, precise, and concrete." She thinks that "the poems seek through a minute and particular observation of the natural world to achieve a dialectical understanding of the tensions and contradictions in human experience"; and the tactile imagery of *Milk Stone* affirms "the contingency and the continuity of human, and especially women's experience" (276–7). Likewise, Wiesenthal praises Lowther's poem entitled "Woman On/ Against Snow," in which Lowther writes,

> Lost as the sun
> among all stars,
> she hears the whole night
> name her,
> Small Small
> Here-by-chance
> Belonging-nowhere-meaning-nothing.
> She says stubbornly nothing
> but poems come from her hands. (*Milk* 15–16)

About the poet herself Wiesenthal comments, "As a 'welfare mother' ... Lowther was fully aware that her poem was as much about the power and prerogative of naming – as 'against' being named – or being nameless – as it was a poem about 'making art'" (265). She regards Lowther as "a writer who grappled continuously with the 'limitations' of her modest experience – and who was sometimes reminded of her 'almost non-existent' biographical small smallness by others" (260). This evaluation of Lowther also applies to the fictional Swann. By comparison, the narrative suggests a reading of Lowther's work as meriting critical attention. If such a reading is intended, Shields performs the cultural and ethical work of commemorating Lowther and reinscribing her in literary history.

A few more examples will suffice to reinforce the specificity of Shields's indirect comparison between Swann's and Lowther's work. Jimroy recognizes that Swann's poems speak to him because they evoke thoughts of "the revolution of planets, the emergence of species, the balance of mathematics" (102). These words recall Lowther's late poems – such as "In the Continent Behind My Eyes," "Riding Past," "Slugs," "Anemones," "Coast Range," and "Notes from Furry Creek" – by emphasizing an interest in astronomy, ecology, and the physical sciences. Lowther's work also employs natural metaphors for a social democratic politics. In "Last Letter to Pablo" she addresses the Nobel Prize–winning Pablo Neruda, for she can identify with his oppression:

> bloodstone
> dark jewel of history
> the planet carries you
> a seed patient as time. (223)

Swann's last verse, "Blood pronounces my name," carries echoes of this poem. The critics speak of her evocation of a "microcosm" (320) and macrocosm of "geo-sociological references" (366), which are equally apparent in Lowther's *A Stone Diary*, a "book that began with the poet making 'blood prints' with her hands on the stones ... all around her" (Wiesenthal 384). It is possible to take critical comments about Swann as allusions to the "relationship between Lowther's own commitments to democratic socialism and ... materialist poetics" (Wiesenthal 375). Lowther herself worked tirelessly as a volunteer and employee at the constituency office of the New Democratic Party. That Shields admired Lowther is entirely possible because of Shields's sympathy and volunteerism with this left-of-centre party (Shields, qtd. in Wachtel, "Interview" 23–4).

Indeed, Swann resembles Lowther as a visionary and a materialist as well as a feminist poet. Perhaps for this reason, Shields's narrator, in the voice of a film director, draws another comparison between poetry and communion, when critics in the final scene reconstruct Swann's poem "Blood":

The faces of the actors have been subtly transformed. They are seen joined in a ceremonial act of reconstruction, perhaps even an act of creation. There need be no suggestion that any one of them will become less selfish in the future, less cranky, less consumed with thoughts of tenure and academic glory, but each of them has, for the moment at least, transcended personal concerns. (396)

Such interconnection is a consistent theme in Shields's fiction and criticism because of its resonance with not only individual, but also collective concerns. *Swann* points particularly to the linguistic and material effects of literary communities. In this way, Shields's narrative demonstrates not only an ironic edge but also a political edge. Throughout the novel a community is most productive, even among critics, when writing is produced from a need to be "fed by all manifestations of sisterhood," as Maloney claims (68). Even the writing of the Cruzzis comes from a shared need to restore harmony in their marriage. Frederic and Hildë Cruzzi make "alterations" to Swann's poetry with "a single hand" (282). In contrast, Jimroy considers the concept of a community of scholars ludicrous, but only before becoming a participant in the reconstruction of Swann at the novel's end. Until this moment, his discourse and attempts to construct the author-function demonstrate his fear of a multiplicity of meanings: to him, as to Foucault, the author is a fixed and "ideological product" ("Author" 209). Jimroy's actions, like the bookseller's, are largely motivated by competition and political interestedness. In the context of cultural politics, Shields's narrative valorizes the woman writer but parodies her critics, and in this valorization lies Shields's political purpose.

Shields's narrative interrogates the author-function in the work of the fictional Mary Swann – and the real Pat Lowther. *Swann* raises questions about the author-function but with a feminist twist. The problems that it poses recall Foucault's: "What are the modes of existence of this discourse? Where has it been used, how can it circulate, and who can appropriate it for *himself?*" ("Author" 210, emphasis added). In reference to women writers, such as Swann and Lowther, these questions also raise the issue of gender as a social category that effects exclusions in discursive and literary practices among critics, including Foucault. The author-constructions of the woman writer in the discourses of Jimroy, Lang, and Cruzzi, and even Maloney and

Hindmarch, are ironized. However, in Shields's exploration of the relationship between author and text, she takes seriously the absence of the woman writer in a feminist critique of literary politics. Both Swann and Lowther assume the role not of the Foucauldian dead man, but of the dead woman in the game of writing. In the critical practices that circumscribe their lives, deaths, and receptions, Swann and Lowther are both erased by the epitaph of *victim*. However, in Shields's critical, ethical, and autobiographical writing, they are honoured and commemorated.

Chapter Three

The Problem of the Body: Romance as Metaphysical Ruin in *The Republic of Love*

In *The Republic of Love*, writer and critic Fay McLeod asks herself this question when she lies in bed at night: how can we possibly speak of love in the last decade of the twentieth century? Fay feels trapped in the language of love, much like her father who thinks of love as "a metaphysical ruin" (319).[1] In this novel Carol Shields turns to romance fiction and its role as a discursive model for women's self-representation. Her novel shows that the dominant discourses of romance and autobiography are, in part, ruined abstractions of language. Shields draws complex connections among books, speech, and self-recognition: "Ordinary life, depending on how we define it, constrains or frees us" (Shields, qtd. in De Roo 47). In the life of Fay, Shields exposes the literary and popular models of romance with which everyday life is invested. At the same time, she does more than parody romance fiction: "I am trying to make a sort of hyper-reality jump [or stand out] ... by writing about love in a serious way" (Shields, qtd. in De Roo 49). By giving her narrative a double twist of irony and urgency, the target of her parody becomes the critical discourse of hyperrealism. She would agree to some degree with Jean Baudrillard's statement that it is "*reality itself today that is hyperrealist*" (147, original emphasis). However, her text's self-reflexivity and its embedded life story expose the romance and, simultaneously, subvert a critical discourse about the hyperreal and the failure of language.

Shields's novel questions dominant discourses of Western individualism and original desire – discourses in which the romance is constituted. Fay and Richard McLeod think they desire only what they have freely chosen but they resemble literary characters, such as Don Quixote or Emma Woodhouse, who imitate romantic heroes or heroines. Shields makes visible what cultural anthropologist René Girard calls the imitative nature of desire (42). Fay's life reveals how romance narratives are intertwined with autobiographical self-representation. In turn, self-representation becomes part of a shared love story, "our story" (278), in which Fay's and her fiancé's lives are interconnected with others' lives. Fay's story also reveals her critical models: her struggle is ideological, since ideology is a way of making sense of the world. However, Fay's romance with Tom Avery is not only a represented experience but also an embodied one. Her story mirrors her parents' stories, too, in the celebration and breakdown of a marriage. The novel's feminist revisionist reading of the self can be seen as an ideological act by which Shields renegotiates and redefines assumptions about women's individual lives and experiences. *The Republic of Love* offers readers both a feminist critique of popular culture and a creative gesture towards an ethical criticism. The novel shows that women's self-representation and evolving criticism can still change lives and engage others. The story of Fay and Tom's romance involves not only a reversal but, paradoxically, a double reversal to renegotiate and renew the metaphysical ruin that is the romance novel.

Literary critic Perry Nodelman misjudges the novel as "not really all that much different from the kind Harlequin publishes" (112). His statement is inaccurate but it recalls a definition of the real as "*that which is always already reproduced*" (Baudrillard 146; original emphasis); identities and self-representations consist of "stereotypes and analytic models" and our attitude towards the world is akin to a reading of it: we live like readers (Baudrillard 121). In other words, the experiences of ordinary life, including romance, are necessarily interpreted according to discursive and generic models. But *The Republic of Love* is not a popular romance; it is a self-reflexive metafiction that calls attention to interactive processes of reading, writing, and interpreting.

In an interview with the *West Coast Review*, Shields raises the same problem as her character. She explains, "I'm trying right now to write a serious novel about love, love between a man and a woman, and have discovered that the language of love has been trivialized in our society" (Shields, qtd. in De Roo 55). The problem is linguistic and the romance is dominated by stereotypes from fiction and popular culture. Still, Shields has no wish "to abandon the material [or language] we're embedded in, but rather to reveal it for what it is – necessary oxygen" (Shields, qtd. in De Roo 47). In her text, she explores life narratives and the body as sites of communication and, as other women's life writing shows, "rich grounds for thinking through the relationship between identity and representation" (Gilmore, *Autobiographics* 84). The body resists representation to the extent that, after having exhausted her self-knowledge and theory, Fay prostrates herself at the threshold of Tom's apartment. Resistance of the hyperreal is possible, as Shields asserts: "Some postmodernists think there is no point beyond the language game, but I think there can be" (Shields, qtd. in Wachtel, "Interview" 44). Theorist Susanna Egan would agree that in contemporary autobiographical practices "the body resists current cultural notions that the self is constituted entirely in language and in text. In part, some resolution of the body-mind dualism results from a cultural paradigm shift that revalorizes the body as a significant component of identity" (5). Fay discovers, too, that "people make new kinds of arrangements ... they renegotiate" (318). Shields's text parodies the romance novel and, simultaneously, presents a feminist critique of the politics of self-representation in relation to gender and individualism.

Shields models her understanding of the writer-critic as one who renegotiates dominant discourses by self-consciously writing "a book about a woman who [is] writing a book about mermaids" (Shields, qtd. in Anderson 149). The mise en abyme emerges most clearly at the end when Shields's book closes as Fay's book is launched. Shields's work renegotiates and reclaims the romance novel and historical elements of the realist novel. Shields performs the role of a writer-critic who thinks in broad literary and historical terms. Some theorists consider the novel form to be in ruins because, as a discursive construct, it represents not the real, but the hyperreal; but Shields reclaims the novel itself in a type of critical intervention. She renews its meaning in the socio-historical context of a growing tradition of women's life writing.

In her criticism as well as her fiction, Shields views the novel as a form that women have shaped from its inception. She thinks that, as a satirist whose purpose was to "convert the fluff of romance into something more nourishing," Jane Austen modified the romance novel (*Austen* 30). Shields recalls elsewhere that Canadian author Frances Brooke published the first novel in North America ("Craft" 150). *The History of Emily Montague* (1769) even parodies and expands the epistolary novel established in England only two decades earlier by Samuel Richardson's *Pamela*. Shields contends that women often experiment by crossing boundaries between fiction and autobiography ("Three" 54). In Susanna Moodie, Shields sees these genres as interrelated because "real events are never freed of personal interpretation or imaginary extension" ("Three" 54, *Voice* 68). She observes that in Moodie's fiction the protagonist, Flora Lindsay, presents herself as a "romantic heroine" (*Voice* 31), just as Moodie does in her memoir *Roughing It in the Bush*.

Shields positions herself, too, in an ongoing tradition of women's writing. For this reason, she reconsiders a critical question: "What does a female literary tradition mean and who gets to name it? I see it as still growing towards its definition, investigating the question of reclaimed language and redeemed experience ... I am persuaded that the popular tradition must be taken into consideration, since it echoes and even interrogates the established tradition, taking liberties, offering models of behaviours" ("Thinking" 12–13). That Shields already had these issues in mind before writing *The Republic of Love* is clear from a review that she kept with her novel's manuscripts (LMS-0212 1994–13 36, f. 7). In reviewing Alison Lurie's *The Truth about Lorin Jones*, she finds the female subject "fey"; she enjoys the biographer's projection on the subject and she discusses the word "heroine" as a "gendered term" ("The Ineffable" 13). While Shields understands postmodern concerns about the death of the novel (Shields, qtd. in Denoon 11), she insists that the form remains alive on the frontiers of experimentation and that the frontier has moved "womanward" (Shields, qtd. in Hollenberg 353). She gestures towards a history of women's writing with the frontispiece of *The Republic of Love*. This image employs many romantic conventions: a bird's-eye view of the fated lovers, an arch of trees to create an enchanted bower, and an obscured vanishing point to suggest the undetermined journey of lovers who embark on a new life together. The caption, "I'd like to put my arms around you," is echoed in the landscape by the interlocking branches overhead. In fact, Shields's dual interests in a tradition of women's life writing and the relation of non-fiction to fiction, stem from her graduate studies and participation in a symposium on nineteenth-century Canadian women writers held at the University of Ottawa in 1988.

Because of a self-conscious grounding in a literary historical perspective, *The Republic of Love* must be read as more than a simple parody of the romance novel. Lorna Irvine finds instead a complex mix of realism and romance that ironizes the language of romance with an "embodied omniscience" (153). If Shields's concern is not the language of romance alone, then a larger concern – and the target of her parody – is the critical discourse of hyperrealism. Shields employs a double strategy of challenging literary and popular conventions, on the one hand, and critical theory, on the other hand. She puts these ideas into the mouth of her female protagonist.

Fay represents her experience with Tom as "a romance," despite her claims that it is "impossible to speak of love in the twentieth century except ironically" and that romantic love is only a "literary device" (250). While researching mermaid myths as the curator of Winnipeg's National Centre for Folklore Studies, Fay thinks that she and all the women she knows are "pleading for a share, a role ... in the pageant of romance" (94). Fay publicly denies a need for love but privately reads nineteenth-century novels for their pattern of "predicament, resolution, a happy ending" (158). An intentional emphasis on intertextuality is evident from Shields's late addition of this reference to nineteenth-century fiction on proofs sent to Penguin's senior editor, Mindy Werner (LMS-0212 1994–13 38, f. 3, p. 21). The narrative arc of a life is a literary model for Fay's self-representation. Like her friend who thinks that life is a story (79), Fay dreams of an almost miraculous correspondence of the real to discursive models. She wishes for the miracle of love to "enter a life and alter its course" (248). However, her story of a thousand and one nights with Peter fails to "add up to something" (6), and with Robin she fears the courtship *"just isn't going anywhere"* (118; original emphasis). In early manuscripts, Robin's last name is actually Bookbinder (LMS-0212 1994–13 36, f. 6, p. 92), probably to emphasize the bookishness of his courtship.[2] Like many people's lives, Fay's life is "a mess" for its lack of a firm shape (80). Her thoughts resemble Shields's comment on life writing: "The only story with a nice firm shape to it is the story of a human life, but so much of it is unknowable" (Shields, qtd. in Wachtel, "Interview" 27–8). Like a heroine in a romance novel, Fay seeks to distinguish herself from ordinary women who exhibit chaotic lives and relationships. She confuses a generalized romantic model with the "particularity" of her sexual desire for Tom (364). As Wallace Martin suggests, "the stories people tell in everyday life are similar in structure and purpose to those in ... literature" (183). Fay sees her error only after she dismisses Tom as a modern-day Bluebeard.

Like Fay, Tom wishes to escape the plotlessness of his own life. Shields's narrative emphasis on similarities between Fay and Tom deconstructs gender differences. In this way, Shields articulates an urgent concern of women writers: to interrogate the "limits of gender as a category of analysis in an effort to sharpen the critical and political edge of feminist criticism, especially insofar as a focus on gender may theoretically diminish the significance of sexuality, race, and class" (Gilmore, *Autobiographics* 11). Instead, the gendered subject can be positioned both "inside" and "outside" the ideology of gender. The feminine subject, Fay, is clearly presented as exceeding categories: she could be described as "a 'woman' who recognizes and knows herself, to some extent, through her culture's gender codes but who can also critique this coding and read gender as a construction" (Gilmore 20). In this way, Shields's narrative and character embody critical practices in women's life writing.

In addition to literary and critical models, Fay is subject to popular models from films and songs. She compares Peter's awkward kisses to those presented in a "silent movie" (40), and she interprets her dissatisfaction as a sign that she has fallen "out of love" (15). She leaves him despite her desire for a baby, a dilemma for which she later cries almost inexplicably. By signalling a gap in Fay's thinking, Shields exposes both the bodily crisis and the linguistic one that can arise from contradictions among contesting discourses: after all, even the desires of motherhood can be seen as culturally constructed. Not surprisingly, Fay cries after attending a baby shower. She finds only a fleeting intimacy with Peter as they sing the Beatles's tune "I Want to Hold Your Hand" (38). The moment cannot, however, change the revulsion in her stomach (5) and distaste for his "teacherly finger" (14) or "pedagogical tone" (26). As a museum educator with an English accent, Peter Knightly resembles Mr Knightley, the pedantic lover in Austen's *Emma*. Fay has outgrown this romantic model at thirty-five, just as Emma's growing self-knowledge corresponds with a resistance to the authority in Knightley's voice ("Fingers" 136). Before Fay and Tom meet, each seeks a diversion in the erotic film *Juice of the Larger Orange* (104); later, when they get together, they drink orange juice repeatedly as though taking true love into their bodies (239, 252, 290). A repeated emphasis on the fleshy fruit and its association with the body represent eruptions of the real into the hyperreal.

Fay's parents share the romance narratives that shape their daughter's desires. Her father, a retired entrepreneur whom she resembles, reads "books about windmills" (130). Like a contemporary Quixote, Richard is a romantic and devotee of love. He encourages Fay's quest for passion, if it is her heart's desire, but he thinks that true love is rare. Her parents' model marriage hangs over her like a spell. Her mother also plays the role of a self-sacrificing lover, though Fay cannot think why. This narrative gap signals gender ideologies that are literary and middle class. Peggy believes that "there's something to be said for having a center, for belonging to someone" (13). Despite her success as a gynecologist and writer, she downplays her ambition for the sake of romance. Fay wants to be "the absolute center for someone else," too, even though she suspects it is "a form of vanity" (108). The discourse of desire is a kind of mirror, like the bathroom mirror into which Fay peers while "puzzling over the disguise of her body" (183). She seeks a unified and stable identity while noting that gender identities are the unstable effects of language: "Bodies dissolved in water. Bodies made of water" (154–5). Shields's critical emphasis is evident from her novel's working title, *Bodies of Water* (LMS-0212 1994–13 37, f. 9).[3] She deliberately foregrounds the body by writing against the grain of traditional autobiography, a discourse from which the body is typically absent.

While Fay is under the "spell" of her parents' marriage, Tom is "enchanted" by his friends' marriages (244, 281). He repeats like a mantra a phrase that he overhears in a grocery store: "Love is the only enchantment. This, he said to himself, is how a Chinese gong must feel when it's struck by a hammer in its absolute center" (70). The narrative underlines the unified self that is produced by romantic discourse, a subjectivity that is a fiction of the real, as Richard discovers to his dismay when his marriage collapses and "there isn't any love left" (319). In the hyperrealism of contemporary culture, the discursive model is a type of "enchantment" (Baudrillard 24–5). After three breakups and three divorces, respectively, Fay and Tom occupy a subject position of disenchantment. Fay professes an individualistic and feminist autonomy: "I, Fay McLeod, have every right to breathe this air, to take possession of this stretch of pavement" (7). But her mouth puckers at the words and an increasing unease belies her self-representation. At times, Shields's narrative undermines Fay's liberal assumptions with a sharp irony: "How fortunate a woman she is to possess this kind of skewed double vision" (75). A contradiction in thinking explains Fay's lie to a colleague that she misses Peter "not in the least" (108). Despite her ambivalence towards the loss of Peter, she claims a feminist autonomy that echoes Beverley's espousal of work and friends in lieu of a husband. Later, Fay wonders what Tom's embrace might mean, and her mind struggles to interpret it, exposing the limits of her self-representation. But her body responds, and they hold one another "in a way that [is] urgent" (201). Fay reflects on the moment when Tom first said, "What I'd really like is to put my arms around you" (197). This climactic moment in the development of the romance is calculated for a maximal effect on the reader before the plot's reversal.[4] By highlighting the physical urgency and mirroring encounter of two lives, Shields subverts autobiography's roots in the eighteenth-century Enlightenment and its ideology of individualism. She uses the romance to develop two subjects in order to question the generic assumption of the singular, autonomous self – and the disembodied subject.

While Shields exposes the limits of Fay's self-representation and liberal assumptions, she reveals the limits – and successes – of Fay's critical practice. Fay authors a paper entitled "Mermaids: A Feminist Perspective." But she asks herself, "Do I believe one word of this?" (97). In her early research, her interest in mermaids comes from an experience with a former boyfriend. He gave her a soapstone figure after accusing Fay of being "impenetrable" (14); she describes this mermaid as "impenetrable" and "asexual" (54). With breasts and a tail like a "ferocious writhing penis" the mermaid is "an emblem of sexual ambiguity" (97), an enigma of female virtue and malice. At stake in any gendered representation is the relation between discourses of power and identity (Gilmore, *Autobiographics* 19); accordingly, Shields's shows her heroine engaging in feminist activities of interpretation and intervention in cultural debates and myths. Fay reinterprets the mermaid as a gender stereotype whose "seductive capacity is valued over her reproductive capacity" (97). From a feminist and embodied perspective Fay's life informs her criticism.

Caught in power struggles personally and professionally, Fay draws the ire of a male critic who justifies his verbal attacks and sexual advances by assuming that her feminine purple dress signifies her availability, arousal, or "engorgement" (97). Clothes can be viewed as material extensions of the body that are open to interpretation. To Fay's mind, the richness of the dress's colour is intended simply to "disarm her critics" (96). Shields's narrator offers another view that reveals what Fay fails to see. Like the mermaid's phallic tail, the dress signifies power; it signals a middle-class identity that intersects with a gender identity. Fay loves her clothes, especially a pink raincoat, just as she loves her china and silverware. By highlighting her gender and class, the narrator shows her complex positioning across multiple identities. With a middle-class identity she differs from working-class women on the bus more than she differs from her male colleague, Peter: "She ... notes with surprise – *but why should she be surprised?* – that those who ride the early-morning buses are mainly women, a separate caste" (58, emphasis added). Initially, Fay denies her bourgeois identity as "vaguely discrediting" (75); later, she admits that a middle-class "reverence for individualism is one of the prime perversions of contemporary society" (267). The narrative demonstrates that an embodied subject is largely, though not entirely, determined by both gender and class.

By presenting a complex critical perspective, Shields's third-person narrator proves to be neither a voyeuristic one, nor a detached camera-eye that might remain "operational on the surface of things" (Baudrillard 143). Hers is not the objective or omniscient narrator of the realist novel who "tells the story but does not indulge in commentary" (Martin 133). Instead, the narrator is a commentator and critic who takes the stance of a feminist revisionist. While frequently consonant with Fay's perspective, the narrator's viewpoint is sometimes distanced from hers for the purpose of the parody. The narrator, who is feminine and subjective but undramatized, parodies individual autonomy, feminine or masculine.

A masculine autonomy is deconstructed by contradictions between Tom's professional image and his self-representation. The broadcaster is depicted as an eight-foot ogre on a billboard for his radio station. When people mention the "humongous" (89) and "fantastic" image (103), Tom senses his alienation from others. The oversized close-up effects an estrangement from his own image, just as a film actor is estranged from his body. The image is "super-real" and "Olympian" (82–3); and Tom associates the caption "he's our boy" with shifting masculinities. He recalls his photographer's comment that the urban male is "paralyzed by Woody Allen-ism" (82). Before his bathroom mirror, Tom reflects wryly that the "business of being a guy ... never let[s] up" (44). He compares himself with the hypermasculinity of television star Burt Reynolds and his thoughts are self-critical: "Hey, you'd better get yourself together" (22); "Smarten up, big fella" (45). He even addresses his penis: "You wimp" (173). Tom's awareness of the instability of gender identities is no less pronounced than Fay's. Shields emphasizes the media images that infect everyday language, including self-talk and self-representation. From the disembodied face on the billboard the narrative shifts to an embodied perspective. Jogging to divert himself from a recent divorce, Tom also runs to purify himself. He wishes to regain the youthful image of his celebrity self. After witnessing a heart attack in a marathon, he sees a doctor about his blood pressure and "weary libido," yet he refuses to discuss it due to his "macho pride" (104). Like a romantic hero, Tom's desire for love is an ache "for something, but it wasn't sex" (105). Work and romance are as demanding as a casual lover, Charlotte, who orders him to bring her to orgasm.

Like the spectacles of the marathon and parade that Tom encounters, the hyperrealism of popular culture invites him to enter "the great festival of Participation" (Baudrillard 139). On a research trip to France Fay similarly encounters a parade. She is "enchanted by the procession" to Chartres, though a bystander calls it "complètement fou" (203–4). Fay muses that the pilgrims' march gestures "toward a world in which responsibility, for the most part, prevails," and in which she is stirred by a "kind of love" even for a strange friar (203–4). The words "kind" and "for the most part" suggest that she lives, like Baudrillard's subject, "in an 'esthetic' hallucination of reality" and nostalgic "proliferation of myths" (Baudrillard 12, 148). But Fay is portrayed with considerable complexity as a critic and "woman plagued with information" (5). At times, the narrator presents her simply as a "receptor of external stimulation" like a mirror or "blank lake" (9). At other times, she resists cultural myths, unlike the two French women who see an eel in a lake and assume it is a waving mermaid. The mirror and parade are tropes of self-recognition and ideological "interpellation" – the process by which "one is hailed as a subject and waves a hand of acknowledgement in return" (Gilmore, *Autobiographics* 20). By depicting Fay as an agent capable of social action, Shields resists critical theory about the determination of the subject.

In her critical practice Fay finds that the mythic figure of the mermaid is both "primitive" (128) and iconic as a "corruption of Christian symbol" (205). When she questions the French women about their sighting, they claim the mermaid was waving to them: "Beckoning. *Appelant de la main*" (208). Suggestive of their ideological interpellation, the wave is the most significant detail of their account and it is repeated in English and French; in fact, the italicized French phrase is added to a late manuscript, indicating the author's intent (LMS-0212 1994–13 38, f. 4, p. 356). Fay knows that the young women's adolescent imagination "prised" the mermaid "out of the available culture" (210). Although the sighting is supposedly confirmed by news accounts, the women admit the mermaid looked like pictures they had seen. Moreover, the lake was "swimming with eels," a fact that calls into question their tale of a mermaid that "looked at first like a net full of eels" (206–7). Fay's conclusion that their story is false is supported by folklorist Hélène Givière's finding that a previously reported mermaid was likely an eel. In comparison to the young women, Fay's own interpellation by critical discourse appears in her response to the "wave of a hand" from critics at a conference in Paris (198). Their dialogue is accompanied by the "fleshly extravagance of arms and lips" that Fay describes as almost "erotic rapture." They express "a longing to become part of one vast undulation. Bodies of the old and young curl toward each other, speaking of commonplace things but signaling desire" (198–9). Shields shows that the critics' words, no less than the young women's, derive meaning from interpretive communities, social practices, and embodied experiences.

One scholar is described as especially hairy and "ripely physical." Taking her hands, he sighs, "Ah, my dear" (199). His words bring to mind George Herbert, the metaphysical poet who in "Love (III)" dramatizes the blissful communion of the Creator and creature. Fay's response *"ravish me"* echoes John Donne in "Batter My Heart," a metaphysical poem that turns on the paradox that only in the bonds of love can one be free. This sonnet stresses a resemblance between sacred and profane loves, a theme to which Shields's chapter title also alludes. The theme is evoked again by a quotation above Fay's desk from Leonardo da Vinci: "Art lives from constraints and dies from freedom" (54). Fay applies his words to love (365); Shields applies them to life (Shields, qtd. in De Roo 47). From such allusive language, we see that Shields self-consciously reintroduces into the text many historical and collective ideas of love, in contrast to the individual love of modern and romantic discourses. She renews the meaning of love as sacramental and embodied: "the visible sign of incalculable trust" (192). She suggests that romantic discourse is like the French "bise" or "buzz" of a kiss "that can mean nothing or everything" (199). The significance of the word "love" is contingent upon a convergence of individual and collective contexts in a particular instance. Shields's narrative implicitly makes the same point about critical discourse. Occurring at the novel's midpoint, the chapter on the conference is pivotal because it presents the unravelling of hyperrealism. Under general circumstances, a confusion of the medium and message can amount to a "confusion between sender and receiver" and their "unlocatable" positions (Baudrillard 76–7). In particular circumstances and from specific locations, confusion can be reversed and meaningful communication restored. Thus, Shields's text resists the notion of the failure of language.

This chapter also marks a turning point in the plot when Fay receives Tom's message that he loves her. She gets it in Paris, the city of love: the sender, receiver, and context of the faxed message are clear. By sending her a letter Tom wishes to "remind her of a novel *she'd* once read" (188, original emphasis), perhaps a romance novel in epistolary form. Her expectations are shaped by the form and conventions of love at first sight. Fay is called upon to respond in kind: "I love you too" (218). These words recall her thesis on the pre-marriage agreement. Though less codified than the marriage vow, the social script offers a similar promise and "exchange of sentiments" (220). A declaration of love is a "private pledge" that is later "broadcast to the wider community" in the publication of banns (221). Mouthing her response as she faxes it, Fay performs a speech act that connects language and gesture. It is also part of a gendered ritual: Fay knows that the declaration is typically "spoken first by the male and echoed by the female" (221). Despite her notion of a mutual declaration of love, romantic discourse is not necessarily democratic – "a republic" – any more than it is "necessarily patient" or "kind," as historical and sacred texts might suggest (224, 1 Cor. 13). Instead, the socially constructed and contradictory positions of the free individual and the gendered subject provoke dreams of being caught, mermaid-like, in a tangled web of language.

Fay wavers between contradictory subject positions, believing herself to be alternately "at rest" and "crazy" (221–2). Likewise, Tom worries about his "crazy words," even though he feels as "sane as he'd ever been in his life" (215). The narrative emphasizes a physical response to Fay's touch in their first embrace. He feels enchanted by "the particularity of her touch" because he trusts her instinctively (196). An expert communicator, he reads "the screen" of her open face and admires her mobile mouth (193). Fay is equally attracted to his lips and wonders "how it would feel to kiss that mouth" (179). Later, in sexual union, she reads him with her hands, drawing them along the arc of his back. She senses "his loneliness coming toward her," and her body responds as if to say "come" (234–5). The coincidence of language and gesture produces an experience of the body as "transparent, fluid" (235). Fay begins to feel like "a woman in love, any woman" (247). Here an emphasis on the general rather than the particular signals Fay's representativeness as a feminine subject of romantic discourse.

After Tom moves into her condo, Fay persists in a romantic belief in destiny. She thinks of love in metaphysical terms, especially the "transcendence" and "miracle of it" (248). Fay insists that a love affair with Tom is her destiny, unlike Iris who stresses physical compatibility. Fay tells Beverley that she is having a romance, and she tells Robin that it is "just something that happened" (250–1). Similarly, Tom clings to a physicist's romantic concept: "Our bodies are made of stardust" (238). As his statement illustrates, even scientific ideas can be "fictions substituted for reality" (Baudrillard 113). Despite her romantic notions, Fay knows that love is founded not on sentiment alone but also on trust. Just as Tom trusts her, she declares, "I trust him" (247). Mutual love and trust are based on exchanged vows, but Fay avoids making promises for fear of breaking the spell of romance. When she does promise never to leave him, Tom is "over the rainbow" (244). The rainbow symbolizes a promise that he associates with their first meeting at a party when she arrived with rainbow-coloured balloons. Tom hopes that she will liberate him from the "panic and capsized faith of the single life" (254), and they agree to marry.

Fay's personal insights into the reciprocity of love inform her critical practice. She resists gender ideologies from the work of two contemporaries. A Freudian critic, Maja van Ginkel, says that "the mermaid trope is identified with the [male] sexual subconscious, with a primitive fear of castration and an urge to return to the watery womb" – an Oedipal complex (182–3). But in the Louvre Fay discovers Egyptian artefacts that depict mermen as well as mermaids. They contradict van Ginkel's thesis, which claims the female figure of a mermaid is the subject of male desire. Similarly, the artefacts contradict the thesis of a French feminist, Gabrielle Favian Grobet, who says that a mermaid is the "archetype of the sea temptress" whose female desire is denied (202). Despite opposed views these critics resemble one another more than they differ: they both use theoretical discourses of desire and universality to assert their authority.

Shields thus parodies the competition and rhetoric of real critics. Although, in reality, Judith Butler criticizes Luce Irigaray, their rhetoric does not necessarily invalidate a shared feminist critique that "culture or the Symbolic is predicated upon a repudiation of women's bodies" (Butler 118). Whether in real or fictional realms, feminist critics need not undermine one another. Fay's feminist practice is expanded by engaging in others' ideas and further research. She finds, as Baudrillard does, that the "artifact is something else entirely than a controlled transformation of the object for the ends of knowledge: it is a rude interference with reality" (123). Fay then questions the uniquely male desire in van Ginkel's thesis: "don't they [people] sometimes commit acts of abandonment, *calling out to each other*, demanding to be buried in each other's mortal or immortal flesh?" (183, emphasis added). She also questions the female desire in Grobet's thesis: "This, Fay decides ... is the mer-condition: solitary longing that is always being ... denied" (203). In purely theoretical discourses she finds a reductive and disembodied subject, whether masculine or feminine.

While she resists gender stereotypes Fay still associates subjectivity or "mer-ness" with the "perfect composure" of a fixed identity (225). The "self-image" that Fay values "above all others" is an individual autonomy: "to sing mournfully to herself" (220). But her assumptions are contradictory. The autonomous self is produced by a discourse of desire that expresses a "fey longing for the inexpressible" (205–6). Fay's self-representation reflects an individualism in which desire and political space are "like two ends of a curved mirror," catching the subject in a "vertigo of interpretation" (Baudrillard 35, 31). She already sees the contingency of mermaid myths, and she has begun to think "she would never get her various theories glued together" in order to write her book (195). In her life and criticism she finds herself "suspended" in a romantic "image" (176). At the same time, such discursive models are more than theoretical structures since they embody social structures. In addition to the web of language, it is the web of social relations that Fay must negotiate.

Upon their engagement Fay and Tom are expected to attend two social events, an engagement party at the Warings' home and an anniversary party at the McLeods'. The former never takes place but Fay takes "the general rejoicing" as a sign of their elevation from the "ignominy" of singleness (260). It is not fate but social spaces that have brought them together. Fay thinks of the city itself as a geographical space and "knowable network" where "families overlap with families, neighborhoods with neighborhoods" (77). She knows that the "problem with stories of romance" in novels and films is "that lovers are always shown in isolation" (333). She and Tom discuss their family trees but their differences exceed their expectations. Class differences prove to be greater barriers than gender differences. At the anniversary party Tom feels like a stranger to the McLeod family. He has never attended a party like this one and he is alienated from Fay's middle-class family. In the familiar role of a disc jockey, however, Tom selects songs from the 1950s to suit the occasion: "A suburban house. An October night. A graceful assembly of friends" (263). Most guests are the McLeods' friends, including Tom's former father-in-law, Foxy Howe. He lives in Tuxedo Park, an upscale neighbourhood, like River Heights where the McLeods live. The geography that is "destiny" is a social space that is encoded by exclusionary discourses of class. Foxy has sent Tom a "box of shit" (127), while Fay's godmother, Onion, simply "reserves judgment" (260). Even Peggy withholds her approval, although Fay wants her to say, "*I adore him. I can see exactly why you love him*" (270; original emphasis). Tom cannot anticipate the family crisis that is precipitated by Onion's absence at the party.

Fay's family differs from Tom's in that his stepfather is a barber and his mother is a nurse without a university degree. She was single and pregnant at sixteen, and, after being hospitalized for postpartum depression, she gave him up as a temporary ward of the state. A social worker in Winnipeg placed him in the university's department of home economics as a practice baby. Tom humorously portrays himself as a sensitive man with twenty-seven mothers, but his ignorance of his father's name is a disadvantage on a university application. A therapist says his second marriage failed because of a "psychic confusion concerning women" in spite of his mother's care (241); the therapist assumes he lacks individuation or masculinity. Gaps in Tom's story signal a silent suffering that is caused by stereotypes of gender and class. His second wife leaves to marry "someone rich" (269). Of his three ex-wives only Sheila keeps in touch because she herself is marginalized as a lesbian. Tom regards his failed marriages as "a string of bad luck" (241), but he ignores the social forces that shape his personal history.[5] Shields portrays him sympathetically as the hero of a competing romantic narrative – in fact, the romance novel historically challenges class constraints in favour of class mobility (Watt 137–8, 162). Shields uses the romance to demonstrate the possibilities and limits of social mobility that persist in contemporary culture.

Tom expects resistance from Fay's family to his social position as a "three-times-divorced disc jockey" (255). Peggy's reservations are echoed by a friend: "I did have some doubts ... I kept thinking to myself, a disc jockey, Fay's going to marry a disc jockey. I couldn't get over it. Not that there's anything wrong with being a disc jockey, but. And his track record, marriagewise, that's another thing" (335). A gap after the word "but" signals a middle-class ideology that goes without saying, and that privileges marriage over singleness and professions over jobs or trades. Peggy's resistance to Fay's engagement brings a silence like her silence about Bibbi's partner who is a shoemaker. Jake's name does not appear on the McLeods' invitation to their anniversary party, while the name of Clyde's wife, a lawyer, does appear. Peggy worries that her daughters "are not 'settling down' in the usual way, marrying, producing children, and investing in property" (131). Fay still hopes that she and Tom can find "citizenship in each other's lives" (247), and Tom cherishes an engagement announcement to "certify his connection to his fellow citizens" (297). The announcement in the newspaper privileges family names and public identities over personal names and private identities, which have greater currency in the romance novel. Fay's competing identities as daughter and lover reveal a split subjectivity corresponding to public and private selves. Eventually her split subjectivity causes Fay to break off the engagement. Because of the breakdown of her parents' marriage and her alignment with her mother, she begins to view Tom as a "dangerous stranger" (332).

Once again, Fay's life influences her criticism when she presents another paper, "Mermaids and the Mythic Imagination." Her talk emphasizes not the gender identity of the mermaid, but the social communities that support the myth. She says that the story of the French women was "widely reported in the press, and these reports ... have validated the vision" (289). By drawing attention to collective beliefs and assumptions, Shields exposes the ideologies to which individuals are subject. Fay assumes that she and her educated audience remain outside the circle of those who believe in myths. In accordance with a liberal ideology she thinks she and her colleagues act as free and objective individuals but these ideas are undermined. Her professional and middle-class biases are apparent in her denial of Tom's wish to attend the colloquium. He is conspicuously absent but her colleagues and friends are present. Fay justifies her exclusion of Tom by stressing the difficulty of the paper's language when she actually fears introducing him to co-workers. Her words and actions betray an exclusionary logic.

When Fay's father abandons her mother, Fay reacts intellectually and physically. Her hands turn cold, her senses are numbed, and her throat is stopped: "There was something here she wasn't understanding. And something, too – the thought came later – something she instantly understood, a skewer driven straight to her brain" (308). Like Peggy whose "heart's been cut out of her body," Fay loses faith in romance. She regards her father's eyes as "opaque with disenchantment" and she sees romance as "a black hole" (308, 320). She suspects the ensuing gap in the family narrative is a "bourgeois black hole" (310). She is troubled by her father's gesture indicating her parents' stories are "irresolute arcs" (318). She is equally troubled by her mother's silence for the sake of respectability: "She's got this idea ... That she doesn't want anyone to know" (312). Tom comes and goes like a stranger while Fay stays in a ruptured household. The conflict of daughterly and romantic identities has material consequences for her and Tom, who is now a "solitary body" (323). By sleeping apart, cancelling the engagement party, and refusing to wear a supposedly unlucky wedding dress, Fay is "systematically dismantling that *thing*, that megachip he's come to think of as his happiness" (326–7; original emphasis). Fay deconstructs the romance, no longer desiring to be married in the church where her parents were married. The narrative foregrounds the body to show that subjectivity is performative and to suggest its contingency. Shields again resists the idea that subjectivity is stable and ideologically determined by dominant discourses.

Fay soon sees her father as a stranger, while her mother believes he shows signs of temporary insanity. His apartment is mean by Peggy's standards; it is near the airport and city limits. Because Richard appears sane, Fay sees him as doing penance for the pain he caused his family. Contrary to the McLeods' earlier belief that to end up alone would be "the ultimate horror" (132), he displays a monkish contentment in a modest brown apartment, recalling the "brown-clad" friar in France whose "maladroit body" Fay loved (204). The friar and Richard redefine the role of a father as something other than a middle-class patriarch. Richard claims he "couldn't breathe," just as Bibbi would have "died" if she had not escaped the smothering love of Peggy (349). A recent retiree, he felt neglected while his wife occupied herself with work and writing a book. His self-representation shows that the romance and the family narrative are, in Rosemary Hennessy's terms, overdetermined and full of contradictions (29). Richard resists his production as a subject through social practices and romance narratives. Hennessy's definition of "the social" applies here to Shields's narrative: "an unstable set of relations in perpetual disequilibrium, formulated in terms of a ... map rather than a system" (18). The course of Richard's life is not determined by the romance novels he and Peggy once read together in bed.

Richard still urges Fay to reconsider the decision to cancel her marriage plans. In contrast, Peggy concerns herself with mundane tasks, such as returning gifts and calling guests: "she performs with the unstudied competence that has made her famous among her friends" (337). She appears composed only in the social practice of middle-class motherhood. Fay is surprised at the difference between Peggy's mothering and loving; she is motivated by something other than Fay's welfare. Fay's body may be safely "enclosed" in her mother's arms each day, but she cannot sleep when it yearns for the comfort of Tom's arms at night (335–6). As she remembers his body a phrase from the marriage ceremony – "*with my body I thee worship*" – takes on new meaning.

Embodied memory begins, paradoxically, to undo the reversal of a decision to marry. Although the family narrative contradicts the romance, the physical and social threat of a bottle of urine changes her mind. It comes by mail, probably from Foxy, who sent feces to Tom. Like excrement, urine stands "for the danger to identity from without" (Reineke 78). Fay also fears the loss of "some inviolable notion she has constructed of herself": the middle-class identity of "nice Fay McLeod" (331). The urine represents the dual threats of identity breakdown and social expulsion, which Fay perceives as being connected to the disgrace of Tom's failed marriages. She faces the possibility of becoming an abject subject that is regarded as *other* and eliminated like excrement. The body itself must be viewed "not as a ready surface awaiting signification, but as a *set of boundaries, individual and social, politically signified and maintained*" (Butler 44, emphasis added). Fay has a feel for the social game, the "intricacies of play and penalty" (39), and she thinks that a penalty is being exacted from her in the delivery of urine to her door (329). Fears of abandonment and exclusion caused her to reject Tom. Despite a conscious decision to leave him, an unconscious "undertow of memory" now creates the feeling that she cannot bear the "cup" of grief that is the loss of Tom (348). The image evokes a communion cup and cup of sacrifice, which suggests Fay has made an unworthy sacrifice for the sake of a class identity.

The double reversal of the romance is completed by a blessing from her godmother. Onion's earlier refusal to attend the McLeods' party hurt Fay, but she corrects her mistake and confirms Fay's error in rejecting Tom. Fay sees that Onion's body trembles at the loss of a long-time lover: "I couldn't bear thinking I didn't belong ... to anyone" (354). Fay heeds the warning of one who tried unsuccessfully to ignore the body's needs. Peggy describes Onion as a self-sacrificing "lamb" (337), who denied herself the joys of a conjugal life. Acting on Onion's insistence that she "do something" to correct her mistake (354), Fay prostrates herself at Tom's door in a reversal of self-sacrifice. She arrives not in her mother's wedding dress, but in Onion's fur coat, resembling a "creature who'd wandered in from the cold" (358). Shields's narrative emphasizes the irreducibility of the body as a referent by refusing to dissolve it in language. As a woman who "sees life in symbolic images," Fay cannot immediately grasp her new self-knowledge as an embodied and "aberrant creature, slumped in Tom's doorway, pleading for admission" (364–5). Shields's emphasis on the body reads as a feminist revisionist strategy, for "the body is located both *inside* and *outside* the social deployment of power" (Hennessy 44; original emphasis). Shields dramatizes in Fay's life a crisis that is both ideological and physical, and that makes possible new subject positions.

The story of Fay's father similarly undergoes a double reversal. By leaving Peggy, Richard has "taken leave" of his senses (316). He has disregarded the physical details to which his wife attended, including his diet and socks. She even visited the ailing aunt who had inspired Richard to act as a model husband. When an airplane wheel suddenly falls through Richard's roof and narrowly misses him, he regains his senses in a traumatic "shock" that reminds him of his "mortality" (364). Fay describes the event as fate; but Shields emphasizes life's fragility. Richard becomes aware of the physical need for survival and the social need to tell another about his experience. He calls Peggy with a request to return home and she says "come" (357). In her response she resembles the beckoning mermaid on the cover of Fay's new book.

Fay's criticism, in a paper entitled "Mermaids and Meaning," is once again influenced by her life. Her desires for "rapturous union" (366) and "lifelong companionship" are fulfilled in the marriage ceremony (358). Her previous desire for love at first sight was the projection of a subjectivity in crisis and "poised for change"; her later arrival at Tom's door dramatized the body's "hunger for the food of love" (366). Shields's emphasis on the latter is clear from a late manuscript, in which she indents the last sentence to make it stand out in a separate paragraph (LMS-0212 1994-13 38, f. 6, p. 615). When Fay marries Tom, the script that is "creased" from repeated use is charged with meaning because of the "particularity" of her desire for him (364). The creased text is a mise en abyme for the narrative fold that becomes the double reversal of the romance: "Love renewed" (364). The narrative fold signals a feminist double strategy that is self-reflexive and political. As Paul Smith points out, "The effect of feminism's double-play is demonstrably to have broken down the old habit of *presuming* the 'subject' as the fixed guarantor of a given epistemological formation, as well as to have cast doubt on the adequacy of the poststructuralist shibboleth of the decentred 'subject'" (151; original emphasis). The text of the marriage ceremony codifies love, *"the most elusive of human bonds"* (359; original emphasis), and yet the words are renewed in a spoken pledge and social contract to which Fay attaches her signature. The marriage text becomes meaningful by engaging the body. In Shields's novel the female body is, in a further twist, reinscribed in a religious discourse; the time frame spans a period from Good Friday to Christmas, signalling a thematic movement from death to life.

The novel ends with the launch of the book that Fay dedicates to her godmother, *Mermaids of the Inner Mind*. Its cover image is a mermaid with one hand beckoning, and the other holding a comb. Fay's book offers a Jungian interpretation of the mermaid as the "anima" or feminine principle, with one hand symbolizing the desire for union, and the other "representing love and entanglement" (366).

In the expanding contexts of Shields's text the mermaid represents, on the one hand, the hailing of the subject and, on the other hand, the female agent's capacity for resistance. Both apply to Fay's action in society as a woman writer. Fay's writing is a gesture and the pen, like the comb, "fits in her hand" (204). Instead of regarding the pen as alien and phallic, as some feminists have done (Gilbert and Gubar 61), Shields views the pen as extension of the female body (204). Her text reads as a political call for a timely re-emergence of women's writing on the historical horizon of Western culture. Shields's work also reads as an ethical call for the individual and collective love of one's "neighbour" (362). *The Republic of Love* concludes with a social vision of responsible citizenship in the lives of others, and a personal vision of an ethical criticism to which women writers contribute. Fay glimpses this dual vision: she understands that she must act upon the suffering and anguish of real "human bodies" (364). For Fay – and by extension the reader – the narrative presents the reversal of a theoretical vision in which hyperrealism wins out over history. In the novel's closing lines, Shields focuses readers' attention on the need for attendance to a shared hunger for the food of love. The rise of the anima signals the rise in social practices of love for the other without their dismissal as womanish.

Chapter Four

The Problem of the Subject: *The Stone Diaries* as an Apocryphal Journal

In *The Stone Diaries* Carol Shields creates a *casse-tête,* or narrative puzzle, that challenges readers' interpretive skills. This novel has in fact generated the most criticism among her books because of sudden and sometimes disconcerting shifts in the narrative voice from the first person to the third person. The question that arises is who narrates this account of the life of Daisy Goodwill Flett, an ordinary woman? Shields offers a clue in an interview by stating, "I was writing about biography"; however, she adds enigmatically that she was "usurping" the genre (Shields, qtd. in Denoon 10–11). Though it is still a matter of debate whether Daisy writes her autobiography or whether an anonymous biographer writes her life,[1] one important detail has escaped critical attention. The opening poem bears the signature not of Daisy, but rather of Judith Downing. Entitled "The Grandmother Cycle,"[2] this poem is evidently intended as an epigraph – a quotation or, in a figurative sense, an inscription on stone – which provides an interpretive frame for the subsequent story. Yet no one has addressed the significance of Judith's signature. By examining its significance we can better understand Shields's larger concern in this novel, which is to challenge perceptions of women's lives and life writing.

To the attentive reader, the signature suggests that Judith writes her grandmother's life story. Moreover, as the narrative itself suggests, it is possible that she works in collaboration with Daisy's daughter, Alice, and her grandniece, Victoria, to piece together Daisy's life from journals, letters, and other sources of which traces are found in the text. The implications of a narrative that is a self-conscious and multiple-voiced construction of a life are profound. Shields's readers would do well to remember Virginia Woolf's adage that "we think back through our mothers if we are women" (83), as Shields does in her essay "'Thinking Back through Our Mothers': Tradition in Canadian Women's Writing" (12). Furthermore, Shields's narrative signals the presence of not only the voice of Daisy but also the voice of another I-narrator, whose political project is to subvert the authority and generic conventions of autobiography by rewriting Daisy's personal history. This reading of the narrative as an apocryphal history, or "apocryphal journal" (*Stone* 118), is supported by archival evidence, Shields's own commentary about the novel and about women's writing, and by textual analysis. In fact, *The Stone Diaries* produces simultaneously resistant readings of gender stereotypes and of the autonomous self, suggesting that both are cultural fictions. The text presents, therefore, a sophisticated and complex feminist critique of dominant discourses such as autobiography, and it anticipates theoretical directions in women's life writing and autobiography studies in recent decades. By comparison, critical arguments about its genre and narrative shifts pale in significance.

With regard, first of all, to the archival evidence, Shields's play upon both the genre and the subject of autobiography is apparent in the evolution of the novel's title and protagonist's name. In the Shields archive, the working title of a draft dated 27 February 1991 is "My Life / by Elinor Goodwill Harris" (LMS-0212 1994–13 40, f. 7).[3] This title implies a fictional autobiography. Significant to my argument, however, is an earlier title, "Elinor Harris: A Life," which implies instead a fictional biography (LMS-0212 1994–13 40, f. 2).[4] Another draft dated 2 October 1991, is entitled "Daisy Goodwill: A Good Enough Life?" to indicate a mock biography or parody (ibid., f. 22, p. 1). On a subsequent but undated draft, the title appears as "Monument: A Life of Daisy Goodwill," while yet another title page reads "The Stone Diaries / A Novel by / Carol Shields" (ibid., 42, f. 7). By the time that Shields signed a contract with the book's co-publisher, Random House of Canada, on 1 March 1993, the novel was provisionally called "Monument," but the title has been crossed out and replaced in ink with "The Stone Diaries" (LMS-0212 1997–04 68, f. 1). Autobiography may be interpreted as a monument to "the self it constructs and that constructs it" (Gilmore, *Autobiographics* 74); therefore, the title "Monument" signals a parody of autobiography.

As the novel's epigraph emphatically states, in a voice other than Daisy's, her life could be called a monument. Although the narrative itself may be read as an autobiography, the text's double-voicedness, from the outset, subverts and exposes the autobiographical form as a simulation of a life. Narrative theorist Shlomith Rimmon-Kenan observes that "self-conscious texts often play with narrative levels [that is, embedded narratives] in order to question the borderline between reality and fiction or to suggest that there may be no reality apart from its narration" (95). This is indeed the case in *The Stone Diaries*, which I read as a metafiction or meta-autobiography. Leigh Gilmore observes, moreover, that the autobiographical space may be regarded as a labyrinth of history and language into which the gendered subject disappears (*Autobiographics* 63). This effect is one that many readers recognize in Shields's text. Even the Goodwill Tower, a monument built by a man with a silver tongue, becomes a trope for the masculinist discourse of autobiography. The tower that Daisy's father builds is described, ironically, as a monument to the absent woman whose body lies buried beneath "the tower's hollow core" (*Stone* 70); it becomes, instead, a monument to himself. The text's autobiographical narrative is similarly exposed as void of the presence of author and subject alike.

As a gendered space, autobiography can nevertheless be resisted and altered, as it is in *The Stone Diaries*. This novel is about the limits of autobiography, as stated in the publisher's blurb on the first edition. The feminine subject, Daisy, is both decentred and reconstructed in a polyphonic narrative. This paradoxical treatment of the subject is significant in that autobiography studies are recently marked by an "interpretive contest" of opposed theoretical positions: "At one end of the spectrum of interpretation, a poststructuralist position ... reads autobiography tropologically and constructs the self as an effect of language ... At the other, a feminist position grounds autobiographical form and meaning in the experiences of the women who write autobiography" (Gilmore, *Autobiographics* 18). *The Stone Diaries* stages this contest for the reader by producing both poststructuralist and feminist readings of the genre and subject. The narrative thus demonstrates the dual purposes of gesturing towards an apocryphal history and valorizing an "ordinary" woman's life. The narrative offers the structural metaphor of the mise en abyme in order to reverse, parodically, the disappearance of the figure of the woman writer.

Many critics correctly identify Shields's text as parodic and metafictional. For instance, it is sometimes characterized as a meta-autobiography (Roy 115), a pastiche (Hansson 355), a parody of postmodern conventions (Billingham 284), or "auto/biografiction" (Ramon 130). However, a second I-narrator exists without being identified by the text or critics, though Christian Riegel posits a second narrator who provides commentary (214). Shields's text thereby displays not only a slight parodic edge (Clara Thomas, "Slight" 109), but also a wry parodic edge. To call it slight is inadequate because it is rapier-sharp: it is tempered only by an ethical reluctance to turn satire on the powerless, as Shields remarks in Austen (*Austen* 32). In interviews, Shields hints at her political project of "writing from the void" by "masking the narrator" (Shields, qtd. in De Roo 48), while remaining "indifferent to the boundaries between literary forms" (De Roo 38). She suggests that "the 'I' voice," far from being identified with Daisy's voice, is actually an intrusion into Daisy's life (Shields, qtd. in Denoon 10). Either Shields is coy or she is unconscious of this narrative effect; but one suspects that she is deliberately coy.

While the I-narrator in the novel's first line may initially appear to be Daisy, the voice shifts to the third person by the second line. In addition to frequent shifts from the first to third person, there are also intrusions of another I-narrator who is largely external to Daisy's personal history. This narrator observes Daisy's birth and stresses the narrative's contingency rather than its determinacy or destiny: "History indeed! As though this paltry slice of time deserves such a name ... *I* am almost certain that the room offers no suggestion to its inhabitants of what should happen next" (*Stone* 39, emphasis added). The second I-narrator is sometimes consonant with Daisy's perspective, but the commentary is often distanced from her perspective and metafictional, emphasizing the text's status as artifice. Wallace Martin describes the purpose of this kind of commentary: "If I talk *about* the statement or the framework, I move up one level in the language game ... the writer has become a theorist" (181; emphasis added). Daisy is no theorist, for "she's been far too preoccupied for metaphysics" (*Stone* 320). But the second I-narrator frequently provides a critical commentary: "When we say a thing or event is real, never mind how suspect it sounds, we honor it. But when a thing is made up ... we turn up our noses. That's the age we live in. The documentary age" (330). The narrator also frequently comments from a peculiarly feminine perspective: "The real troubles in this world tend to settle on the misalignment between men and women – that's *my* opinion ... But how we do love to brush these injustices aside" (121, emphasis added). In this passage the reader encounters an I-narrator who questions literary and cultural conventions, especially the binary opposition of feminine and masculine genders, and who exaggerates the formal characteristics of autobiography in a self-consciously parodic way. Readers also glimpse the second I-narrator in the statement that "irony haunts the existence of Daisy Goodwill Hoad, a young Bloomington widow ... who's still living in the hurt of her first story, a mother dead of childbirth, and then a ghastly second chapter, a husband killed on his honeymoon. Their honeymoon, *I* suppose *I* should say" (122, emphasis added). This statement is parodic and metafictional, for "whenever the 'fictional narrative/reality' relation becomes an explicit topic of discussion – readers are removed from the [generic] framework normally used in interpretation" (Martin 179). Other glimpses of a second I-narrator appear throughout *The Stone Diaries* in statements such as these:

> The doctor – whom I am unable, or unwilling, to supply with a name – announced bronchial pneumonia. (74)
>
> How much of her available time bends backward into the knot of their joined lives ... To be honest, very little. There, I've said it. (230)
>
> That's Daisy for you ... In a sense I see her as one of life's fortunates, a woman born with a voice that lacks a tragic register. (263)
>
> She lies there thinking ... and attempting to position herself in the shifting scenes of her life. Her life thus far, I should say. (282)
>
> Isn't there anything else you can tell me? (348)

The intrusions of the second I-narrator increase in frequency towards the end of the novel, as though intended to be progressively self-revealing.

These intrusions of an unnamed I-narrator represent ruptures in the autobiographical pact, an implied social contract between the narrator and the reader. The "autobiographical pact" is a term coined by Philippe Lejeune, the father of autobiography studies, who also notes that autobiography presupposes an identity of name among the author, narrator, and protagonist ("Pact" 12–13). Even a fictional autobiography assumes the identity of the narrator and protagonist. However, *The Stone Diaries* subverts the generic convention of monologism with dialogism. While the second I-narrator is not the subject of her own story, she is a narrator-participant in the story. Because this I-narrator does not give her name, the text falls into a generic "zone of indetermination" and it becomes a game of ambiguity with the reader ("Pact" 19). Different readings of the same text can coexist, and this uncertainty stimulates theoretical reflection on the part of the reader. Because Shields's text allows the reader to oscillate between autobiographical and biographical readings, the text becomes a generic hybrid. The generic ambiguity, in effect, affirms the text's fictionality while it valorizes the life of an ordinary woman.

The generic mystery grows as the perceptibility of the second I-narrator becomes increasingly overt, particularly in the ninth chapter when the I-narrator describes a hospitalized Daisy: "She's lost track of what's real and what isn't, and so, at this age, have I" (329, emphasis added). The ambiguity has been heightened consciously, as a corrected draft in the Shields archive reveals:

> Does Grandma Flett actually say this last aloud? I̶'̶m̶ She's not sure. I̶'̶v̶e̶ She's lost track of what's real and what isn't [next text inserted:], *and so, at this age, have I.* (LMS-0212 1994–13 43, f. 6, p. 334; emphasis added)[5]

The changes are not, however, in Shields's handwriting, as her script appears in other drafts, but rather in an editor's handwriting. The corrected draft follows a cover letter with the letterhead of "Hazel Coleman / Editorial Services" at "14 Lower End / Piddington / Bicester / Oxfordshire / OX6 OQD" (LMS-0212 1994–13 43, f. 4). Dated 17 March 1993, the letter is addressed to Christopher Potter, Shields's editor at her London publisher, Fourth Estate.[6] These changes represent, then, Hazel Coleman's editorial decision to make overt here what Shields implies elsewhere in the text. From the absence of any attempt by Shields to restore the original wording, one can only assume that she approved of the changes. Shields certainly approves of similar changes in another interview. She also reveals an editor's hand in clarifying the text's hierarchy of voices: "In this book I fell into using parentheses by the thousands, and my editor Christopher Potter ... suggested I look at that again. There's a sort of *undervoice*" (Shields, qtd. in Joan Thomas 56; original emphasis). Furthermore, Shields explains that Daisy is not writing, but rather thinking her story. She emphasizes that in the novel there is a mise en abyme, or "box-within-the-box, within-the-box" structure (58), in which Daisy's story is embedded. In other words, Daisy is not the only recorder of events in *The Stone Diaries*.

The double-voicedness of the narrated monologue or thought also stands out in the final chapter: "Stone is how she finally sees herself ... [She] feels herself merge with, and become, finally, the still body of her dead mother" (358–9). Again, the present tense is added by Coleman, presumably to heighten the immediacy: "Stone ~~was~~ *is* how she finally ~~saw~~ *sees* herself" (LMS-0212 1994-13 43, f. 6, p. 371; emphasis added). The autobiographical effect is, moreover, heightened by a quoted monologue that sounds like a voice from the grave: "I'm still here, inside the (powdery, splintery) bones ... I'm still here, oh, oh" (352). This passage and its parentheses appear in Shields's early notes for the novel, indicating the authorial intent of drawing attention to the narrator's presence (LMS-0212 1994-13 40, f. 1, p. 42).[7] The use of parentheses creates what Dorrit Cohn would call the "fleeting specter of a fictional narrator" (63). Shields claims elsewhere that she values fiction for its ability to go where biography cannot: inside the head (Shields, qtd. in Wachtel, "Interview" 27–8). The doublevoicedness, or polyphony, accounts for the reported thought, the commentary, and the many authorial intrusions throughout the text. In a particularly overt comment regarding Daisy, the narrator says, "Her autobiography, if such a thing were imaginable, would be, if such a thing were ever to be written, an assemblage of dark voids and unbridgable gaps." For the most part Daisy is "erased from the record of her own existence" (75–6). This comment, among others, draws attention to the narrator's writing process, as the epigraph also does.

The epigraph frames the narrative in such a way that the signature of Judith suggests that she, not Daisy, writes this life story. Taken from the poem "The Grandmother Cycle," the epigraph characterizes Daisy as a woman who never said "quite what she meant" but whose life "could be called a monument." These lines indicate that Daisy is the text's subject, rather than the speaker, and they raise many questions. The epigraph prompts the reader to ask, who is Judith Downing? Evidently, Shields's editor asked this question because in the Shields archive, among the novel's manuscripts, are proofs from Fourth Estate with Shields's handwritten note after Judith's name: "a minor character in [the] novel" (LMS-0212 1994-13 43, f. 4).[8] On this corrected copy and in an earlier version of the poem (LMS-0212-1994-13 42, f. 7, p. 1),[9] Judith's name stands out emphatically on a separate line, not in a parenthetical attribution as it appears in the published novel. The title of the source is punctuated, moreover, with a forward slash as *"Con/verse Quarterly."* From Shields's note and emphasis, we may take the epigraph as a framing device and a parodic one: a "con" verse. From the family tree on the subsequent pages, it is apparent that Judith is Alice's daughter and Daisy's eldest granddaughter. The reader may ask, who would write about Daisy's life, if not a daughter or granddaughter? The name Judith, or Judy, appears not only in the epigraph, but also throughout the narrative with references to her infancy (228), christening (242), gift (331), and adoration of her grandmother (332, 343). Furthermore, she is present when Daisy visits Alice in London (284), and when Alice visits Daisy in Sarasota, Florida (339). In the latter instance, Judith's presence becomes clear only in retrospect. The narrator remarks, "Grandma Flett knows she rambles ... she repeats herself, and Alice, bless her, never stops her, never says, 'You've already told *us* about that, Mother'" (339; emphasis added). Judith and her children are all named in Daisy's obituary, too. Judith has access, of course, to her mother's memories and to Daisy's papers, which are in the possession of Alice and her siblings after Daisy's death. It is most likely Judith who records the closing chapters and who is the source of the second-to-last chapter's resounding question: "What is the story of a life? A chronicle of fact or a skillfully wrought impression?" (340). The narrator self-consciously foregrounds the practice of women's life writing as a creative gesture and ethical act of commemorating a life.

Another question that the reader may ask is this: what would motivate Judith to write Daisy's life story? The final chapter, which is full of unanswered questions about Daisy's life, provides several clues. Many questions follow the discovery of Daisy's papers by her family. Alice reflects, "What I can't figure out is why she never told us about this first marriage of hers" (350). Evidently, Daisy's daughter knows very little about her mother's early life, including her match with the rich Harold Hoad. She also asks, "Do you think her life would have been different if she'd been a man?" (353). Her siblings ask more questions about Daisy's former editor: "Remember Jay Dudley?" and "Do you think they ever ... got together?" (354). The narrator similarly inquires, "Isn't there anything else you can tell me?" (348). Her question echoes Alice's demand in the preceding chapter: "Just tell me how I'm supposed to live my life" (326). These questions convey the family's urgency and desire to recover Daisy's personal history. The ostensibly biographical narrative of the final two chapters strongly suggests that many questions about Daisy's life persist among her descendants after her death and that these questions motivate the narrator to reconstruct Daisy's life.

Read retrospectively, as a biography by a family member, the narrative of *The Stone Diaries* fills in gaps in Daisy's life story – including her first marriage in the fourth chapter, "Love," and her mid-life affair with an editor in the sixth chapter, "Work" – as though in answer to Alice and her family's questions. Read chronologically, however, the life narrative appears to be full of holes. For this reason, critics who view the novel as Daisy's autobiography get caught up in questions about Daisy's reliability or unreliability instead of addressing more productive questions about perspective, narrative strategies, and the narrative process, especially what Wallace Martin calls the "retrospective character of all narrative" (78). The process of interpretation itself is a retrospective process. It is reasonable, then, to think that the narrative concludes with an account of its genesis; in the words of Dorrit Cohn, it is a "circuitous *recorso*," like Marcel Proust's *A la recherche du temps perdu* (76). The mysteries of Daisy's life and its lessons are left for her successors – and her readers – to uncover.

The process of retrospective interpretation finds a fitting figure in the final chapter where Daisy's signature is, in effect, erased when no one thinks of having daisies at the funeral, but only pansies. The daisy is, after all, recognized as a kind of "signature" in embroidery on her lingerie and part of her legacy (*Stone* 350). Although the reference to the pansy evokes passivity, it also evokes an active surrogate mother, Clarentine (77), who was a member of the Mothers' Union and part of the turn-of-the-century movement for women's suffrage. The flower imagery – and by association a woman's name and signature – subverts feminine stereotypes to signify women's agency. It symbolically reverses the erasure of Daisy and her predecessor from the historical record.

But if Daisy's signature, which in effect would guarantee an autobiographical narrative, is not self-evident, whose is? Judith is the most likely candidate, but her mother, Alice, must also be considered. Daisy's final words, "'I am not at peace'" (361), are set off by double quotation marks, once again indicating a double-voicedness that signals the narrator's presence in reporting her thoughts. A possible clue to the narrator's identity is found in the literary allusion of these final words. In part 4, section 3 of Fyodor Dostoyevsky's

Crime and Punishment, the phrase "I am not at peace" appears in the context of an autobiographical narrator's frustrated ambition (282). This allusion suggests that Alice, a scholar of Russian literature, influences the narrative. Other allusions, such as the imagined return to childhood (337), the kidney (357), the "mouth in a little round circle" (355), Daisy's "oh, oh" (352), and the meditation on death, echo another Russian novel: Leo Tolstoy's *The Death of Ivan Ilyich*. It is also significant that Alice takes Daisy's name by changing her own name from Flett to Goodwill: "Flett was a dust mote, a speck on the wall, standing for nothing, while Goodwill rang rhythmically on the ear and sent out agreeable metaphoric waves, though her mother swears she has never thought of the name as being allusive" (325). Alice, rather than the "literal-minded Daisy" (321), must also inspire the reflection on names in the preceding pages: "That's all – just Daisy Goodwill ... cutting off the Flett and leaving the old name – her maiden name – hanging in space, naked as a tulip ... She cherishes it" (320). It is probable that the reflection is shared with Judith because the description comes from the granddaughter's perspective: "A secret rises up in Grandma Flett's body" (320). Alice, the failed novelist, is in the process of rewriting her own identity; indeed, she is thinking back through her mother.

Alice is also a diarist, who is disillusioned with both feminine stereotypes and cultural notions of autonomous selfhood. She has burned her old diaries but she can still recall her youthful idealism. After her first year of college she claimed to have altered her life in a day, simply by plastering over a crack in the ceiling that seemed to her a sign of destiny and a prescribed feminine identity: the crone (231). When her mother is in fact perceived as an old "hag" (335), Alice contradicts this gender stereotype but without smoothing over its effects. Her rethinking of her mother's life undoubtedly influences Judith. Alice's views of her mother and identity are everywhere apparent in the narrative, especially in the dialogue and letters, ranging from a belief in Daisy's "latent ability" to write (210) to her belief that Daisy's "death" actually occurred while she was "still alive" (342). Alice's perspective particularly dominates the fifth chapter on "Motherhood," when she helps Daisy with a meal, resists her mother's explanation of sex, recalls her cousin Beverley's first visit, and takes the lead in conversations with her siblings. Alice is the probable source of the family consensus that Daisy has been "crowded out of her own life" by the gender role of a mother (190).

In Alice's portrayal, Daisy exemplifies the growing alienation of women from the postwar cultural ideal of the self-sacrificing wife and mother, as illustrated by Betty Friedan's *The Feminine Mystique*, a favourite book of Alice (242). With its publication in 1963, this book marked the beginning of second-wave feminism. Daisy's experience is evidently interpreted through the lens of Friedan's work.[10] Significantly, it is Alice's photo that appears three times in the family album even though Daisy's image is absent.

While it may be argued that Alice is the biographer-narrator, several factors suggest otherwise. Although Alice appears to be the opinion leader in the family, she is not always presented in a favourable light but focalized from a critical distance, suggesting that she herself is not the narrator of the text. For instance, the reader is told that "Alice is discouraged at the moment" because of her failed novel (325), and that "from her middle-age perspective, [she] believes her mother to have a soul already spotless – spotless enough anyway" (332). Ironically, she almost canonizes Daisy; a biography by her alone would resemble hagiography. The narrative provides a critical view of Alice; therefore, she herself is a focalized subject and not the sole narrator of *The Stone Diaries*. Instead, she must be regarded as influencing or collaborating with Judith, who is thinking back through her mother, just as Alice has done, and Daisy before her. There is no singular perspective in this text.

In addition to Alice, Victoria may be a participant in the collaborative writing of Daisy's life. Near the end of the novel, there is a description of the diarist Daisy as "Day's Eye" (339), her witnessing eye opening daily, like the flower for which she is named. This poetic description again signals a narrator's artful intervention in the text by recalling the opening chapter, when the eyes of Daisy register the sensation of her first breath as if to say "open, open" (40). In contrast to the newborn baby whose mother dies in childbirth, witnesses to her birth are "borne up by an ancient shelf of limestone" (39), like the supporting arm of a mother. The paleobotanist, Victoria, is the probable source of the limestone imagery that functions as a mise en abyme for the narrative in its entirety. The subject, Daisy, is embedded in cultural and family narratives, just as fossils are embedded in limestone. Even in the final chapter, the description of Daisy's metaphorical merging with her mother in a rock formation recalls "God's Gate" (300), a geographical feature that Victoria observed on a trip to the Orkney Islands with Daisy. In fact, the eighth chapter, "Ease," is told largely from the perspective of Victoria, incorporating many details about the life of her own mother, Beverley, who conceived her out of wedlock and who was supported by Daisy. Victoria's participation in the narrative would also explain the inclusion of her children's photos at the end of the family album, a textual clue that has gone almost unnoticed.

For Judith, Alice, and Victoria, reconstructing a woman's life necessarily involves a process of interpretation, particularly in the selection and ordering of events and the representation of the subject. Together they produce an apocryphal history and thereby seek to restore a woman's life to the historical record, an impulse that animates a great deal of postmodern revisionist history, especially among feminist revisionists (McHale 90–1). The unauthorized biography is, then, compiled by Judith, whose very name alludes to a writer of apocrypha. Daisy is said to feel as though she were part of an "apocryphal journal" (*Stone* 118), a term coined by the narrator. The narrative begins autobiographically with an opening statement in the first person: "My mother's name was Mercy" (1). But it subsequently oscillates between the first and third person. Simone Vauthier notes correctly that the narrative is only "purporting to be the autobiography of Daisy" ("Ruptures" 177), but it is incorrect to assume that the narrator is anonymous (185). It is Judith who, in collaboration with other women in her family, constructs an apocryphal journal and deliberately plays with generic ambiguity.

With the assistance of Alice, and perhaps Victoria, Judith must reconstruct her grandmother's life from multiple sources, the traces of which are found in the text. At the novel's end, "the papers are all there" in her estate (*Stone* 350). Even earlier, the narrator indicates, "Let it be said that Daisy Goodwill has saved every one of Barker Flett's letters" (145), from his early correspondence to his last letter to her. The text refers elsewhere to Barker's private journal, which, though pompously written, discusses Daisy's lost letters to him (111–12). His journal becomes a source for much of the content in chapters two to five. In their retirement, Barker and Daisy are advised to write an autobiography (163) and diary (262), respectively, and Daisy keeps a notebook even in her final illness (323). There are traces, too, of Daisy's travel journal that records her journey to Niagara Falls and a visit to Barker in the fourth chapter: "'I feel as though I'm on my way home,' she wrote in her travel diary, then stroked the sentiment out, substituting: 'I feel something might happen to me in Canada'" (132). Although Hilde Staels assumes that the diary is lost (122), the reader is told only that it disappears for Daisy after she marries Barker. He is the one into "whose hands it may have fallen" (156). He must have kept it because the diary is quoted exactly: "'In one hour I will be there,' Daisy writes in her travel journal, underlining 'there' three times" (150). There are traces of yet another journal, which Daisy kept as a young woman and which she gave up after her second marriage: "Daisy Goodwill's own thoughts on her marriage are not recorded, for she has given up the practice of keeping a private journal" (156). Journalling was probably her chief occupation during nine years of widowhood after her first marriage, when, the reader is told, Barker wonders, "What did she *do*?" (154; original emphasis). Daisy's journals are evidently the sources of her observations about Cuyler, such as his speeches at her graduation and wedding, as well as her reflections on her first marriage, her private conversations about her virginity, and her memories of her childhood, especially the accounts of her pneumonia and Clarentine's stories. All are recorded from her perspective and often in the first person.

It is possible to infer, therefore, that she has similarly recorded an oral account of her birth in a journal, which is quoted extensively in the first chapter. Daisy herself would have had letters by Clarentine, Cuyler, and Barker to draw upon. Furthermore, she would have had *The Skutari Tales* because the biography of the peddler who discovered Mercy in childbirth is listed among the books in Daisy's estate (355). As a personal history that is compiled by his grandson (37), this biography also functions as a mise en abyme for *The Stone Diaries*. It is perhaps no coincidence that in an essay Shields describes a similar book entitled *Ruby: An Ordinary Woman*. It consists of diary extracts that were "rescued by a granddaughter and put into print" ("Narrative Hunger" 31). Here Shields's interest seems to be piqued by a narrative strategy that resembles her own. In a review for the *Boston Globe*, she calls *Ruby* an important cultural artefact and a view into a life that bridged the Victorian and modern eras. Similarly to *Ruby*, which spans the years of 1909 to 1969, *The Stone Diaries* spans the period of 1905 to 1985, and both books reveal the cultural and historical forces that shape a representative female life.

Other possible sources for the narrative of Daisy's life include Magnus Flett's books and "family papers" (*Stone* 96), which, though left in a train station in Thurso (140), might have been retrieved and inherited by his only living relative, Daisy. There are also newspaper accounts, including those that document the popular appeal of the Goodwill Tower (53–4) and letters from friends and family, including Beverley (201) and Fan Flett (179), Victoria's mother and grandmother respectively. The entire sixth chapter, "Work," is constructed from letters to Daisy. Daisy is the probable source, too, of the family tree at the front of the text. After Victoria discusses women who record their genealogies, Daisy becomes "preoccupied" with her forefathers, and having read "a few works of social history, memoirs, [and] biography," she resumes her life writing to recover "a bag of buried language" (266). The genealogy clearly reflects Daisy's perspective because a question mark appears for her date of death while none appears for Emma's, whose survival is uncertain but about which "no one says a single word to Grandma Flett," even when Emma dies (340). Like autobiography, the genealogy represents the knowledge of a life and its trajectory. Unlike autobiography, however, the genealogy represents not only the life of an individual, but also a family narrative. In this respect, the genealogy stands as yet another mise en abyme for the entire text. It is not a traditional autobiography but rather a family narrative, a strategy of other postmodern novels, such as Gabriel Garcia Marquez's *One Hundred Years of Solitude* and Michael Ondaatje's *Running in the Family*.

As a deliberate blend of fact and fiction or "a fabric of substance and comity" (*Stone* 266), the narrative signifies not only a poststructuralist notion of the impossibility of autobiography, but also a feminist notion of thinking back through one's mothers. This apocryphal journal, therefore, offers a resistant reading of autobiography and a feminist critique; it is the political project of Judith, who rewrites her grandmother's history, beginning with Daisy's journals. The text strategically becomes a "discourse of re-membering" that is "written against the language of privation" (Gilmore, *Autobiographics* 90), just as Daisy's journals consider "what can be shaped from blood and ignorance" in her mother's story (23). While Daisy directly influences the text, her gaps and silences are interrogated through embedded narratives in a self-conscious "pattern of infinite regress" (*Stone* 281). Judith's narrative incorporates multiple perspectives and framing devices. The genre of autobiography itself is a framing device that has historically ensured women's absence. At the same time it becomes, as Gilmore argues, a "stage where women writers ... may experiment with reconstructing the various discourses – of representation, of ideology – in which their subjectivity has been formed." On this stage, the feminine subject is "already multiple, heterogeneous, even conflicted, and these contradictions expose the technologies of autobiography" (*Autobiographics* 85). Paradoxically, the gendered space of autobiography into which the feminine subject disappears is made visible by parody. Judith's parody is especially evident in the exaggeration and contradiction of feminine stereotypes.

The simultaneous production and resistance of gender stereotypes becomes the structuring principle of the entire narrative. In "Birth," Daisy is no orphan girl, but she is the abandoned daughter of Cuyler. The orphan is a romantic icon in the fictional autobiography of *Jane Eyre*, which Daisy's adoptive mother reads. Like Jane's, Daisy's mother dies in childbirth but her father still lives. He is present at her birth in 1905, "invited to participate in a moment of history" (39), but, like Abe Skutari, he considers birth to be "women's business" (259). Cuyler abandons her to be raised by Clarentine, while he builds the monument that establishes his reputation and identity. From Clarentine's letters to Cuyler, one learns that the child Daisy looks incredulously at his photo: "Is that truly my father?" (54). Cuyler is able to forget her just as a journalist forgets what happened to the baby (59, 73). He comes for Daisy only when he sees a benefit to his career at the Indiana Limestone Company in terms of gaining respect as a family man. Unlike Cuyler who becomes "a public person" (85), Daisy lacks "the kernel of authenticity" (75). The narrator's sympathy for Daisy's perspective is nonetheless apparent, for instance, in the judgment of Cuyler as "a parent who had surrendered her to the care of others when she was barely two months old" (90). Daisy's identity as an "orphan" obscures her father's responsibility for her disadvantaged start in life.

In "Childhood" Daisy is a daughter but not the daughter of those who raise her. Daisy thinks of her adoptive mother as "Aunt Clarentine," and her guardian as "Uncle Barker" (75). Though Daisy was left "in her charge" (47), Clarentine apologizes to Cuyler for leaving with the child for her son's home in Winnipeg. Her motivation is twofold: first, Daisy would "thrive more readily under female care," and, second, Clarentine "loved your dear wife Mercy with all my heart" (50). Clarentine's letters and stories are obvious sources for Daisy's portrayal of Cuyler's passion for Mercy: "I love you and with all my heart" (16). In contrast, Clarentine leaves a brutish husband to establish a new life for herself at forty-five. Raising Daisy on the income from a florist business that flourishes during the First World War (113) and that is supplemented by Barker's support and Cuyler's allowance, Clarentine is productive and "cheerful" (75). Daisy plays happily in the Eden that is her adoptive mother's garden. Daisy supposedly dreams in her old age of a return to the timelessness of Clarentine's garden (337). The narrator distances the reader, however, from Daisy's perspective on a "golden childhood ... Warmth, security. Picnics along the river. A garden full of flowers" (148). These nostalgic and romanticized self-representations are to be taken with a grain of salt. Many years later when a cyclist-turned-millionaire builds a conservatory as a monument to Clarentine (188), Barker is invited to the opening, not Daisy. She is unacknowledged as Clarentine's adoptive daughter.

In comparison to her relation to Clarentine, Daisy's relation to Barker is more ambiguous, for she is both wife and child to him. Rumours suggest that he is not at the war front in 1916 because "he is the sole support of his elderly mother and a young niece" even though he is "not a true blood relation" (43–4). Despite the "legends that romance around him," he is a frustrated scholar and ascetic (45). For him money is "a never-ending source of distress" (52). His "guardianship" (73), though never "formalized" (149), breaks down after Clarentine's death especially once the sexually repressed Barker notices "the sweetness of [Daisy's] form beneath the sheet" (68). Daisy interprets his strange leer as indigestion, just as Mercy interpreted her pregnancy as "indigestion" (5), but the narrator notes "her uncle's long brooding sexual stare" (77). Barker is later described as "the male god of her childhood" (191–2), to whom she returns as a woman of thirty-one in search of security: "She is traveling to Barker Flett as to a refuge" (146). Her romantic self-representation may be inspired by her reading of *Jane Eyre*, a book that is found in her library (355). She can in fact no longer live in her father's house after his remarriage to a woman of twenty-eight who is younger than his daughter (127). When Daisy and Maria become rivals in managing the household, Daisy seeks a new home. She resembles her mother, whose goal in marrying was to gain a house to "run as she pleased" (33). Daisy sees that she cannot go back and she demonstrates female agency in creating a new identity as a homemaker within the constraints of what is "possible" for a "woman on the verge of middle age" (147). She recalls Barker's attraction and acts on it, as a woman who, in the economic constraints of the 1930s, "recognized the value of half a loaf" (33).

In "Love" Daisy becomes Barker's wife, not niece. Although her marriage to Barker appears as "incestuous" in 1936 (155), he is neither her uncle nor her stepfather. Still, Cuyler recognizes Barker as a father figure who is "almost as old as I am" (156). He accurately predicts that Barker, a senior civil servant, will be "away from home a good deal" and will "dampen passion." In "Motherhood" Daisy is unable to climax in sexual relations with Barker (191–2); evidently, she has never heard the words "I love you, Daisy" (345). He admits in a final letter that "we have almost never mentioned the word love" because of "the disparity of our ages" (198–9). Nevertheless, he does provide a house and a garden that Daisy considers her creative outlet and "dearest child" (195–6). Daisy finds more satisfaction in her creative acts than in her motherly duties. While making meals she is found muttering more than mothering.

In contrast to her marriage with Barker, Daisy's first union is brief. In "Marriage" she remains a virgin but not a frigid bride. Daisy is married but the union is unconsummated (125). Her tie to Harold Hoad ends on a honeymoon in France in 1927, when he falls drunkenly to his death from a hotel window. Despite his "movie star" good looks (124), he proves to be more "toad" than prince (350). His alcoholism stems from his father's suicide, which his mother romanticizes as a "sacrificial act" (110). Daisy believes that she can change him, and she carries false guilt for her inability to keep her husband from drinking; consequently, she withholds from friends the fact that she sneezed before he fell even though it is irrelevant. She does, however, tell Fraidy and Beans that she is a virgin, as a doctor confirms and confides to a mother-in-law who labels her frigid (126). Publicly, Daisy's image as a tragic heroine fosters a sense of failure and "wherever she goes, her story marches ahead of her" (122). Privately, however, she is free of social expectations to marry and she actually enjoys nine years of tennis, gardening, and journalling.

In "Work," after Barker's death, Daisy is a widow again but she is a merry widow. Once again she reinvents herself. She starts a career at a local newspaper by taking up her husband's garden column as "Mrs Green Thumb" in the 1950s and 1960s. Her agency is revealed in letters from the editor in which he responds to Daisy's offer to cover a tulip festival (202).[11] She returns the cheque for her first column, however, because she fails to understand women's right to equal pay for equal work. Daisy is so engaged in her writing that she thinks "very little" of her deceased husband (230), and she reorganizes her household to support her new occupation. When her divorced niece becomes pregnant, Daisy hires her as a typist and live-in housekeeper. Daisy persuades Beverley to keep the baby despite warnings from friends. By acting unconventially, she herself follows Clarentine's model. Victoria later comments, "This was in 1955; hardly anyone kept their babies back then" (270). Beverley gratefully adds, "Aunt Daisy saved my life" by "giving Victoria and me a home" (250). While working, Daisy conducts an affair with her editor until he ends it: "I could see she had a more permanent arrangement in mind" (254). Ironically, Dudley lives up to his name by proving to be a "dud" as a lover, and after nine years, Daisy loses her garden column to a male rival who uses his seniority as leverage with the editor. Dudley adds insult to injury: having dumped Daisy, he patronizes her by saying that she is "taking this *far* too personally" (227; original emphasis). Her rival is equally insincere: "I hope this disagreement won't interfere with our friendship" (227). The injury stays with Daisy until her dying days, when she tells Alice that her rival was killed by an upset vending machine in a strangely poetic justice.

In "Sorrow" she falls silent and is seen as a victim of depression, not injustice. She has no recourse to appeal her job loss. The word "depression" obscures the social causes of a wrongful dismissal. Daisy is deprived of a public identity as a columnist. Early socialization predisposes her to self-sacrifice and a feminine goodness that is almost "stupidly good" because it "cannot cope with badness" (229). As a result, Daisy is unable to escape an "aura of failure." Gossips label her melancholic or menopausal, while the narrator focuses only on her anguish and "suffering" (230). Family and friends offer various explanations for Daisy's so-called breakdown, but neither Alice's feminist view of thwarted ambition, nor Fraidy's Freudian interpretation of sexual frustration can fully explain Daisy's grief. Joan's story of a silent rage comes closest, but even she betrays the romanticism of a victim politics in saying that Daisy embraces an "ecstasy" of "exquisite wounding" (252–3). Daisy is silenced until she reinterprets herself as a retiree among a welcoming community of women in Sarasota, Florida.

In "Ease" Daisy joins the blue-haired set but she is no idle gossip. In the 1970s, she becomes an old crone but she is neither wise nor unwise. She stays active and resourceful. She supports her grandniece's education, calls her children weekly, corresponds with her grandchildren, and plays bridge with her friends who call themselves the "Flowers." She reads, travels, and researches the family tree. She even constructs an unconventional genealogy to resist patrilineage by including surrogate mothers, such as Clarentine, Bessie McGordon, and herself. She is still aware of her marginalization, for "she belongs to no one" (281). A woman's identity is like an inverted family tree, as she once imagined her bronchial tubes in adolescence, when she first perceived her lack of "authenticity" in the public domain (75). She reinterprets her past by keeping "a diary like Virginia Woolf" (262) and by commenting on documentary materials, such as a photo of Clarentine's rhythm and movement club. She creates "an edited [and] hybrid version" of her life story (283). Her life writing leaves memories and traces of language: "the coded dots of life" (301). Like a biographer, too, she traces the footsteps of Magnus to the Orkneys. She portrays him as a fellow "wanderer ... with an orphan's heart and a wistful longing for refuge" (305). After touching his hand and doing some "conscious revisioning" she feels renewed – that is, "young and strong again" (307). Whether she retrieved his papers or only imagined his story (139–40), her writing is seen by the narrator as carefully crafted, hammered, and "reworked" (307), like Cuyler's and Magnus's masterful stonecutting or Victoria's award-winning archaeology.

In "Illness and Decline" she is senile but sometimes lucid. Daisy is called a sweetie-pie, honey, and pet (310, 322), but she considers these labels "reductive" (329). She keeps a private notebook and contemplates her face in the mirror, the mirror and face being tropes of the autobiographical self-portrait. She prides herself on her social graces and courtesy, though the narrator sees her good will ambivalently as an inability to be "the cause of injury" to others (334). This trait is, paradoxically, her greatest strength and greatest weakness. Even when she is "gaga, a loon" (335), she remains open to others, like a daisy turned towards the sun. She finds in the hospital a supportive community of doctors, chaplains, nurse's aides, and visitors, particularly Judith and Alice. She needs an interlocutor – or "at least one witness" – to keep "her life in order" (339–40). It is important to note that a witness biography, or its fictional counterpart, has elements of autobiography (Cohn 29). Daisy's life supports many others, including the scholar Alice (345), musicologist Warren, paleo-botanist Victoria, and the unemployed Joan who is no less valued in the eyes of Daisy.

In "Death" Daisy is no saint. One would assume that after a long life, Daisy must rest in peace, as Warren asserts at her funeral. How-ever, the narrator contradicts him: she is merely silent and her last words are "unspoken." The narrator says that only in the sleep that precedes death does Daisy realize "the injustice of this" silence (345). Just as the stereotypes in previous chapters are contradicted, the monolithic image of the woman as a saint is contradicted, for she is not at peace. Daisy apparently drew upon a social script of a feminine "goodness." But the narrator resists hagiography to create instead "a history indicated through absences" (Gilmore, *Autobiographics* 21) and life narrative that resists dominant identities and genres.

By its consistent contradiction of gender stereotypes, the narra-tive becomes a site of resistance. It resists the genre of autobiography in which "both the self and history are overdetermined as 'male'" (Gilmore, *Autobiographics* 35). At stake in Judith and her family's parody, as in other women's life writing, is "the relation between discourses of power and identity" (Gilmore, *Autobiographics* 19); and together they expose the limits of dominant discourses and identi-ties. For Judith's generation, in particular, the life narrative becomes "a moving target of ever-changing practices without absolute rules" (Smith and Watson 7). Judith's implied readers are, in all likelihood, Daisy's other granddaughters who are represented in the last pages of the family album that occupies the centre of the text. The autobio-graphical space is used, then, not to trace the development of a uni-fied self or narrative voice but to represent interconnected selves, as well as multiple voices and identities. Contemporary autobiography is often characterized, as Susanna Egan observes, by a polyphonic dialogism in order to raise questions about cultural representations of subjectivity (19). Many women writers, though not exclusively women writers, deliberately problematize the genre or, like Shields, blend it with fiction because the novel is an already dialogic genre. Shields's text functions as a meta-autobiography, a form that "fore-grounds interaction between people, among genres, and between writers and readers of autobiography" (Egan 12). While represent-ing the interaction of Judith and her family with Daisy's life writing, the text exposes the "self" as a construct and the autobiography as a fiction. The spin of a double parody is the "torque" that Shields intentionally puts on the autobiographical narrative in this complex novel ("Arriving" 250).

The authorial intent to subvert generic boundaries is revealed by yet another level of embeddedness in the text. As the archival evidence also demonstrates, material from Shields's own life is incorporated into the text. Shields includes in the family album photos of her daughters and perhaps the sister to whom the novel is dedicated. Together with a photo of Shields's son, these images fill the final page of the family album. The photo of the toadlike Hoad, Daisy's first husband, is ironically a baby picture of Shields's husband, Donald Hugh Shields (LMS-0212 1994–13 45, f. 2).[12] Most importantly, Shields also includes in the text many details from a journal that is written by her own mother. The "Trip Diary of Inez Warner" records a retirement trip that resembles Daisy's journey in the eighth chapter, "Ease."[13] Warner travels to England from her home in Sarasota, Florida, just as Daisy does. She visits her daughter, Carol, before taking a grand tour of the United Kingdom, just as Daisy visits Alice. Warner writes of limestone quarries in Yorkshire even as Daisy does in the Orkneys. She observes flowers and gardens and bridge games, all interests of Daisy. Shields posthumously commemorates her mother, further blurring the boundaries between fact and fiction.

It is also evident from the archives that collaboration is a writing practice of Shields herself. She consults with columnist Louise Wyatt[14] and Blanche Howard, a novelist and friend whose comments appear on a draft manuscript dated November 1992.[15] For instance, Howard comments on "Sorrow": "A wonderful description of depression and its mystery, a great exposition on anger (*as we've talked about*)" (LMS-0212 1994–13 42, f. 4, p. 1; emphasis added). She also remarks on one of the few inside views of Daisy in "Motherhood," when she "is touched by a filament of sensation linking her to her dead mother" (190). Howard observes, "I'm so glad to have this insight into Daisy's mind. I know you have distanced us deliberately from her, but lately I've found that frustrating, wanting to know more about this woman who is the binding thread of the novel" (LMS-0212 1994–13 42, f. 3, p. 37). Comments from Shields's daughters also appear on the manuscript. Anne and Catherine Shields approve the sections in "Motherhood" that are written from the perspectives of Daisy's children, Alice and Warren. To one of Alice's letters in "Work" Catherine adds "please send my red cardigan" (212); and in "Childhood" she inserts, "Who made this lemonade?" (77; LMS-0212 1994–13 41, f. 24,

p. 43 and f. 26, p. 20). That remark, which appears in the published text as the previous one also does, draws attention to a narrator who records what the subject does not know. Moreover, the remarks "perfect" and "wonderful" appear on the manuscript beside references to the female body, such as "the silkiness of her inner thighs" (100).[16] These references emphasize the body and its desires, casting them in the materiality of language, even though the body is typically absent from autobiography. Meg Shields comments "HA!" on a reference to *The Flintstones*, a favourite television show of Daisy's grandchildren (299); similarly in the novel, Alice replies "Ha" to Daisy's ironic comment about needing "open-heart surgery on her head" (335; LMS-0212 1994–13 41, f. 27, p. 35).[17] Clearly, Shields's daughters are an intended audience of the novel's parody. Catherine's note on the children's discovery of Daisy's first marriage – "wouldn't these daughters think this very romantic/tragic?" – prompts Shields's expansion of a discussion between Alice, Joan, and Warren (350–1; LMS-0212 1994–13 41, f. 22, p. 10). By engaging in such collaboration, Shields incorporates intergenerational perspectives and language in the narrative.

As a feminine subject that is embedded in the autobiographical and fictional discourses of a polyphonic novel, the subject, Daisy, subverts the generic conventions of a unified self and voice. From the orphan to the old crone, Daisy is presented as having multiple identities that are socially constructed; from the diarist to the columnist, she is presented as having multiple voices. Daisy is represented as a discursive self, or subject-in-language, to parody the autobiographical subject and to subvert the authority of a masculinist discourse. Daisy is a decentred subject whose words are embedded in the life narrative of a second I-narrator, but she is also a performative subject and a female agent whose words to some extent shape her life. Her life narrative is, at the same time, shaped by the words of others, particularly the collaborative writing of Judith, Alice, and Victoria. In this respect, Egan's observation about meta-autobiography applies to Shields's text: "Precisely because no single 'authorial "I"' would control perception, the ironic reader would be more fully implicated in the text ... Because the perceptions being established would destabilize each other, they would also confirm each other" (2–3). By employing the double parody of a meta-autobiography, Shields ultimately valorizes women's life writing and the life of an ordinary woman. Daisy's life is represented from the dual perspective of exhibiting multiple identities and of having survived them. In this type of life writing, as Marlene Kadar contends, one narrative "unmasks the master narrative of history" while the other constructs a survivor narrative and generates hope for the future ("Ordinariness" 130). These are the effects that Shields's text has on the reader who is open to women's life narratives that are at once unconventional and intersubjective or interactive. Rather than a postmodern impulse, the text ultimately demonstrates an ethical impulse: "What a narrative such as this makes plain is that the life genres are not only in flux but that they fluctuate because of an ethical imperative to represent tropes of surviving a gendered economy, in an unjust representation of history" (130). The narrator underscores the injustice of gender constraints in the final chapter (*Stone* 345), emphasizing the political urgency of her narrative. By rewriting Daisy's life in the form of an apocryphal journal, her granddaughter Judith, daughter Alice, and grandniece Victoria commemorate a life that has nevertheless been "shaped in a slant / of available light." It is a life that is interconnected with the lives of others, not a monument to an autonomous male self.

Chapter Five

The Problem of the Subject of Feminism: *Unless* as Meta-Autobiography

Shields's final novel, *Unless*, focuses attention on the life writing of Reta Winters. Reta refers in her journal to women's autobiography as a "feminist structure" (93), a view that reflects her position as a second-wave feminist. Unlike Reta, Shields blends autobiography with metafiction in a sophisticated parody to distance readers from the I-narrator. The Muslim woman – who is unnamed and whose death by self-immolation is the obscured centre of the text – remains veiled by Reta's autobiography, but only until she is finally unmasked by Shields's parody. Shields deliberately uses narrative strategies that distance the reader from Reta in order to rethink the subject of feminism. By creating a crisis-driven autobiography and by placing it within the parodic frame of a mise en abyme, Shields transforms the subject of feminism into an object of inquiry.[1]

Wendy Roy praises *Unless* as "Shields's most explicitly feminist novel" ("*Unless*" 126),[2] but some critics object to the opposition of Reta to the Muslim woman as the other. If the Muslim woman is Reta's double, as Hilde Staels claims, she may indeed be seen as Reta's "'Other' feared self, weak, powerless, wordless, out of control" (128). In other words, on the level of Reta's autobiography, the text reinscribes the privileged position of the first-world woman while silencing the third-world Saudi woman. But on the level of Shields's parody, the text questions Reta's interpretation and appropriation of the other's story. The novel's parody involves "a woman writing about a woman writing about women writing" (*Unless* 269). However, this mise en abyme shows more than a postmodern concern with the problem of authorship. It also shows more than a feminist preoccupation with women's silencing;[3] in fact, the novel's relation to feminism is enigmatic, ambivalent, and ironic. In a complex narrative strategy, Shields experiments with the mise en abyme to resist autobiography by exploring the possibilities of the "arc of a whole life when it curves" (Shields, qtd. in Maharaj 11). That curve occurs when Reta loses a daughter to the street, a crisis that decentres the autobiographical subject. Shields thus creates a narrative space to re-examine the feminist subject; at the same time, she deconstructs notions of identity and the autonomous self. In this way, Shields becomes not only a writer but also a theorist, positioning herself as a writer-critic, with the greatest degree of urgency.

Shields's embedded critique is in alignment with third-wave feminism's call for a critique of *woman* as a category that is historically constructed and open to reinterpretation. The universal figure of a woman can erase race and class differences among women. Judith Butler argues, for example, that *woman* may be understood as a site of contested meanings even in autobiography: "I do not believe that poststructuralism entails the death of autobiographical writing, but it does draw attention to the difficulty of the 'I' to express itself through the language that is available to it" (xxiv). It is precisely the difficulty of the "I" to which Shields draws readers' attention in *Unless*. Her portrayal of Reta as a supposedly representative subject is parodic and her parody is subversive. Far from being a unified or autonomous self, the subject is multiple, discursive, performative, and, most importantly, interconnected with others.

Shields's subject in *Unless* is multiple and fragmented by design. In her crisis, Reta contemplates the "smashed" self-image that she once called "happiness" (1). Her self-perception is mirrored in her novel: "Alicia was not as happy as she deserved to be" (15). Ironically, Reta and Alicia's pride mimics Roman's masculine sense of "entitlement" (258). Also shattered is Reta's identity as one of the so-called lucky ones, who are "healthy," "loved and fed," and "clear" about their sexual orientation (224). But no amount of luck[4] can make Reta forget a daughter who begs at a busy intersection in Toronto. Norah becomes an "outcast," a word signifying the opposite of the Old English "*wearth*" and the root of "*worth*" (12), implying that Norah is somehow worthless. Conversely, Reta is a recognized author and translator of the memoirs of Danielle Westerman, whose 1949 book, *L'Ile*, established her own celebrated identity as "the only feminist in the world" (102). The French title, which means "island," is doubly allusive, referring to Simone de Beauvoir and John Donne to suggest that no woman is an island, just as no man is an island. Danielle calls Reta a "true sister" (8) and insists that they share a common identity as "two women *au fond*" (103). However, Reta's identity as a woman intersects with multiple identities: she is white, Western, middle class, and heterosexual, like Tom and her writing group, except for Annette who is black and Gwen who is lesbian. Danielle herself is bisexual. Shields's text offers a perspective of which Reta is largely unconscious. Reta represents a liberal feminist who, like many others from the 1970s, is "defined through an (invisible) hierarchy of social differences that takes for granted class privilege, values white over black, and sutures her as a sexualized female firmly within a hetero-sexual symbolic order" (Hennessy 110). The represented "self" is by no means unified.

Clearly, Shields's subject is discursively and historically con-structed. Reta recalls "listening to Helen Reddy singing 'I Am Woman'" (57), locating her in a second-wave feminism that peaked in the 1970s.[5] As a university student she encountered Danielle, the "girl-woman who invented feminism" and with whom she now col-laborates professionally. Her private and public identities are located in Danielle's discourse, which, in turn, derives its authority from "allusions to early [first-wave] feminism" (101). Shields exaggerates and marks the notion of gender as mimetic or naturalized by rep-etition.[6] For instance, Reta repeats Danielle's words "goodness but not greatness" in order to define *woman's* experience but she feels as though she has swallowed an eel whole (115). Far from being natural or easy to digest, the category of *woman* is at times alien, at least as Danielle defines it. In the same way, Reta, the "sixties child," can-not understand Norah, the "nineties child" (127). Because women's lives are interpreted through discourse, and discourse is considered as ideology, Shields's narrative gives Reta an ideological context, just as Reta's narrative gives her character a genealogical context (139). But the implied author, Shields, is more sophisticated than her char-acter. Reta naively wonders, "How far back does a novelist have to go in order to stabilize a character?" (140). Shields clearly knows that the discursive subject is unstable. Her subject is located not only in feminist, but also liberal discourses of the 1970s, like Tom's (72). Both are "*soixante-huitards* in spirit" (57) and they have refused to marry since they met during the sexual revolution. They believe in saving the earth and creating "a home of your own," and they are obviously bourgeois (185–6). Their beliefs and values differ from

Danielle's, for she cannot understand the "hierarchy of concerns" (178), by which Reta values the well-being of her family over others' welfare. Danielle does perceive, however, that "women have been enslaved by their possessions" (63). In the end Danielle suspects that Reta has "abandoned the 'discourse'" (224), and thus feminism as a political movement despite its goal of liberating women. Shields's parody exposes Reta's contradictory subject positions in contesting discourses.

Evidently, Reta is a performative subject as a woman and a writer. A wife and mother of three, Reta compulsively cleans her house and counts the "bodies to be fed" so often that she has anxiety dreams about empty fridges even on book tours (85). In fact, Butler's observation about the performative subject may be glimpsed in Reta's example: "what we take to be an internal essence of gender is manufactured through a sustained set of acts, positioned through the gendered stylization of the body" (xv). The subversive repetition on Shields's part shows how gender is open to self-parody, as Butler remarks of other women's writing (187). As a writer, Reta is again depicted parodically: "*The charming Mrs Winters slips on her comfortable beige raincoat*" (35; original emphasis). The description of her appearance in a writerly trench coat is repeated, and in author interviews she must "perform again and again like the tuned-up athlete" (29, 30, 83). Like her middle-class and feminine identities, her identity as a writer carries a "suggestion of impermeability" (34). Here Shields plays on "imperméable," the French word for "raincoat," in a bilingual pun. Both Reta's middle-class and writerly identities mimic masculine identities. Implicitly, Shields's critique explores the totalizing effects of a masculinist discourse while remaining, to borrow Butler's words, "self-critical with respect to the totalizing gestures of feminism" (18–19). Reta performs a feminist practice that is still evolving in her fiction. Ironically, the first book that imitates romance novels is entitled *My Thyme Is Up*. The second book, *Thyme in Bloom*, responds to Norah's criticism that the first novel "might have been a better book if [she'd] skipped the happy ending" (81). Reta's record of self-development is sincere, but Shields's parody is never far from view because "sincerity's over" (29). Almost comically, Reta perches on her "Freedom Chair" (64), plotting her character's fate within a feminist discourse, yet the third book will take a more open form (320). She has only begun to write it at the end of *Unless*, suggesting the circularity of the text in which Reta's story is embedded. Shields thereby demonstrates the ongoing process of rewriting feminist practice and history.

The performativity and discursivity of the subject are further demonstrated in Reta's struggles with her editors. The editor of her first book, Andreas Scribano, is an "old-fashioned man" who values the written word "perhaps too worshipfully" (105–6), and he tells Reta to write another romance novel to distract herself from her present crisis. When they meet at his office, a hierarchical relationship is emphasized by a difference in the size of their chairs, his being a "big father bear chair" while hers is "little" (176). The editor of her sequel, Arthur Springer, later meets Reta in her home but he invites himself, so the relationship of editor to author remains hierarchical. He urges Reta to write "quality fiction" (280), by which he means the novel "form in [a] universal aesthetic sense" (241). At the same time, he demands a shift in perspective from Alicia's to Roman's point of view. Springer acknowledges Alicia's goodness but he favours Roman as "more than good" (267). He sees Alicia's male counterpart as uniquely heroic and capable of complexity, interiority, and the search for identity. Because the French word for novel is "roman," the name Roman suggests that a masculine perspective defines the novel form. Springer insists that Roman is the "moral centre of this book" (285), but Reta rightly argues that the only reason for denying Alicia this position is her gender. The feminine subject, Alicia, becomes a site of contesting discourses. Reta and her editor reach an impasse of opposed – and relative – points of view, and Shields exposes the binary opposition of masculine and feminine perspectives. In addition to revealing this binary division as the assumption of a male editor, Shields shows the stranglehold of identity politics on feminist thought and emphasizes the limiting effect of dominant discourses on her subject and her readers.

Her complex feminist critique demonstrates a political concern that is far greater in scope and purpose than a postmodern concern about subjectivity or language. Her goal is to intervene in the politics of self-representation and cultural productions of the real. For this reason, Shields resists an overtextualizing of social relations. Within social relations that are present and hierarchical, the act of writing itself is stressed as work that resembles housecleaning (44). Like the rooms of the house that are cleared by her labour, the novel becomes a "reclaimed space" for Reta (259). From housework to writing, social arrangements in which women remain de facto an underclass can be transformed by the action of women to change the daily lives of future generations. That action must be individual and collective.

Shields's foregrounding of work and the family narrative emphasizes the subject as not only multiple, discursive, and performative but also – and most importantly – interconnected. Reta's mother-in-law, a widow whose feminine identity defines her "uncoded otherness" (270), is isolated much like an island, recalling the title of Danielle's *L'Ile*. In her life story, as Lois tells it to Arthur, the doctor's wife resists her identity as a housewife by her reluctance to do housework and by her creativity as a baker. In the postwar era Lois resisted being defined by an ethnic identity by referring to her German honey cake as Swiss (298). Still, her desire to be recognized for her creativity went largely unfulfilled. Despite winning a blue ribbon, she succumbed to depression in the past when her husband disregarded her achievement. In the present, she succumbs to silence again when her granddaughter disappears. But Reta ignores Lois's story, failing to recognize in it a woman's active resistance even before the "feminism of the early sixties had ... ignited" (59). Reta's own mother also lapsed into silence, a type of withdrawal or "inversion," rather than a subversion of social roles (218). Shields creates an intergenerational family narrative that presents history as an uncanny repetition of women's silencing. Reta's narrative subordinates Lois's story to hers; thus, Reta's agency is brought into bold relief against Lois's silence.

Reta's individual agency becomes clearer and more suspect in relation to Norah's silence. Both Reta and Danielle shout at Norah because they fail to understand her subject position as a woman of a new generation. Danielle speaks to her "as though through a megaphone, calling her foolish and misguided, a stupid girl who is keeping her mother from getting ahead with her work" (104). Reta tries unsuccessfully "shouting into her face" (131) or using "force" to get Norah off the street (213). Like the psychiatrist who tells Reta that Norah exercises her individual "freedom" by living on the street (214), Reta mistakenly believes that Norah has "*chosen*" to panhandle (42; original emphasis). She thinks that Norah has dropped out, just as her father once did in the student protests of the 1970s. Alternatively, she thinks that Norah is depressed, though Tom insists that Norah is manipulating them for cash (217). Yet Norah has become an outcast who is "alienated from [her] family and from society" (220). Neither medical nor liberal interpretations of her situation can entirely explain the present crisis. As Hennessy remarks, "the notion of 'choice,' so embedded historically in the humanist ideology of the 'free' individual, cannot simply be invoked within a postmodern theoretical framework" (74). Shields complicates the experience of both mother and daughter as she troubles the notion of autonomous selfhood. Reta must admit that neither her thoughts nor her body can be disconnected from Norah "even for a moment" (104). Shields's feminist critique recognizes that consciousness is ideologically produced and she uses interconnected subjects to emphasize the mutuality of the self and others.

As an interconnected subject, Reta views her daughter from the position of middle-class motherhood. She claims the authority of a mother's voice: "All I wanted was for Norah to be happy; all I wanted was everything" (113). However, even the desires of motherhood can be seen as culturally constructed and politically interested. Reta's subjectivity becomes increasingly unstable due to the conflicting desires of love and greed, which correspond to contradictory subject positions in discourses of gender and class. Reta seeks Norah's happiness and fears Norah's exclusion from middle-class privilege since she quit university. This privilege is symbolized by the silk scarf that Reta buys as a gift for Norah's eighteenth birthday: "The scarf became an idea ... Solidity and presence were what I wanted" (89). At the same time, the scarf is "brilliant and subdued" – that is, feminine. Reta thinks a privileged feminine identity is what Norah is "owed," though Norah does not see herself as necessarily "deserving" (89). Although her middle-class parents met at a human rights rally in Toronto's Nathan Phillips Square, it is in this very public square that Norah questions her rights after encountering a self-immolating Muslim woman in a scarf of an entirely different kind. Hers is the "burka" (118), not the silk scarf that "every chic Frenchwoman wears" (87), including Danielle and Reta. The present crisis is an ideological one. "How did this part of the narrative happen?" writes Reta. "An intelligent and beautiful girl from a loving family grows up ... her mother's a writer, her father's a doctor, and then she goes off the track" (13). This family crisis exposes the political interestedness of Reta's narrative. Her desires are the effects of discourses of class and Western individualism, including second-wave feminism, yet the limits of these discourses are concealed from her view. Her eyes are "curtained over" (58), and her blindness to the exclusion of others, such as the homeless or the

Muslim, from many human rights and privileges throws her reliability into question.

Shields's text focuses attention on Reta not as an object of desire, but as a subject of desire. Her desires are often contradictory or imaginary. She professes a love for others in public spaces, such as the library, but only for "fellow citizens" (45). The brick house that she inhabits offers only a façade of stability or "authenticity" (49). She admits to a weakness for luxuries, like the house or the silk scarf, revealing not care for others but "the big female secret of wanting" (98). Her confession, "I want, I want, I want" (47), reveals a split subject that is contradictorily positioned in discourses of feminism and consumer capitalism. But Reta is only partially aware of the contradiction: "We are ... reaching out blindly with a grasping hand but not knowing how to ask for what we don't even know we want" (98). Conversely, the traumatized Norah begs on the street with an open hand.

Reta's split subjectivity is parodically mirrored in her fiction: both Alicia and Roman want love and autonomy, though she is unwilling "to award them what they haven't the wit to define" (189). In the act of writing Reta discovers not only her "lost children," Norah and Alicia, but also "the poison of the printed page" – the "pharmakos" that is the concealment of metaphysical desire (16). Cultural anthropologist René Girard argues that desire is neither spontaneous nor original; instead, it is an imitation of imaginary desire that is derived from romanticism and individualism especially the "illusion of autonomy" (42–3). Girard applauds novelists who expose the imitative nature of desire just as Shields does: "Ridiculous word, *desire*" (*Unless* 188; original emphasis). Reta's discovery of this poison is traced in a journal that is less about self-development, and more about self-representations that go beyond autobiography. The text's meta-autobiography makes the writing process not one of self-formation but rather "*déformation*" (46). Reta's journal leads her to conclude, "I am still I, though it's harder and harder to pronounce that simple pronoun and maintain composure" (197). Instead of using autobiographical discourses as sites of identity construction, Shields uses them as sites of cultural critique about the effects of dominant discourses on her subjects.

Although Reta's journal paints a self-portrait, Shields's meta-autobiography reverses the figure and the ground. As a result, the reader perceives the subject's political and historical contexts that are suppressed in a traditional autobiography. In *Unless* the figure, which is the subject, gives way to the ground of political and discursive processes. Reta is situated in a post-9/11 context, after controversial election results and an apparent failure of democracy in the United States. Reta's paranoia about "planes crashing" raises the spectre of a traumatic historical moment when Muslims become targets of racial profiling as potential terrorists (77). Despite the politically charged atmosphere, Reta hears the Muslim woman's death only as background noise, until the story involves her daughter. Then Reta's self-development yields to a meditation on the other: "This is monstrous ... that George W. Bush exists ... that people are booking flights for their Christmas holidays ... that I am calmly wiping down the kitchen counters" while Norah is on the street (196–7). Reta raises an important ethical question: "what really is the point of novel writing when the unjust world howls and writhes?" (224). Her question echoes another one that is posed by a traumatized Norah: "what is the point?" (129). In the post-9/11 context, the search for identity can no longer be "the central moral position of the contemporary world" (*Unless* 281), nor can the autobiography be a "monument" to the autonomous self (Gilmore, *Autobiographics* 74). Shields's text self-consciously performs an interrogation of Western discourses of individualism including women's autobiography.

In *Unless*, the meta-autobiography ultimately draws attention to political and social connections among crises, trauma, and marginalization. Norah's bent head only appears to exclude "everything around her" (180). Implicitly, Shields's text offers a feminist critique of the kind that Hennessy seeks in third-wave feminisms:

> If feminist history is to address the ways exploitation and oppression shape the social construction of difference, it cannot be a narrative that clings to identity politics. Putting "plurality in the very structure of our theory" means we will have to radically *re*-structure that theory to make *connections* between and among domains of the social. Making these connections has the disruptive potential not only to challenge but also to reimagine the subject of feminist praxis, from an identity or a coalition of identities – which keeps the boundaries between groups, regions, social formations intact – to a collective global standpoint. (Hennessy 136; emphasis added)

Shields's foregrounding of these connections is evident even from the title of *Unless*. The conjunctive adverb *unless* is "the lever that finally shifts reality into a new perspective" (225). It provides a "trapdoor" to "the reverse side of not enough" (224). The reader recalls that Reta's crisis begins with Norah's perception that her love for the world is "not enough" (128), and the same might be said of Reta. Eventually she realizes, "Novels help us turn down the volume of our own interior 'discourse,' but unless they can provide an alternative, hopeful course they're just so much narrative crumble" (224). It is significant that Shields emphasizes an alternative "course" rather than alternative discourse: the statement is a call to responsibility and social action. Even the chapter titles that are conjunctions, adverbs, and prepositions signal her narrative strategy of revealing ideological connections between individual and collective realities.

In terms of individual realities, Shields's text consistently connects the Muslim woman with Norah. She wears a burka (118); Norah wears a scarf (181). She immolates herself in downtown Nathan Phillips Square, whereas Norah begs on a busy corner at Bathurst and Bloor. Like hers, Norah's perceived motive is "self-sacrifice" (249). In an instance of foreshadowing, Reta worries that her daughter's "life has been burning up one day at a time ... and she's swallowed the flames" (65). In some respects Norah and the Muslim woman are more alike than different. In terms of collective realities, too, Norah resembles the Muslim woman. The homeless and the foreigner are social outcasts who must live "outside the realm of cheques and banks and signatures" (217). Figuratively, Norah bears signs of the victim because she is poor and a woman. Literally, her handwritten sign bears the word "goodness," which repeats cultural fictions of feminine goodness and which is associated with passivity. Against the grain of such cultural fictions, Reta writes her novels and letters about Norah's boycott on reading "in the name of goodness" (165). By emphasizing "GOODNESS" in capital letters (12), Shields's parody emphasizes feminine identities, which Hennessy calls overdetermined by "ideological, economic, and political spheres of production" and which reinforce social hierarchies (30). Shields makes visible the connections among these spheres in *Unless*. As critic Margaret Steffler points out, "When the reader converses with the fragmented Norah and fragments of the 'other' woman, there is a fluidity that expands beyond the limited views of the characters and the feminist stance insisted on by Reta" (241). Reading their silences becomes urgent.

The Muslim woman is best interpreted not as Reta's double, but as a silent figure of the scapegoat. Girard's theory of scapegoating and mimetic violence sheds light on her position in literary and social terms. A scapegoat is often a guiltless victim of unconscious collective violence. A sacrificial logic is at work in collective violence and encoded in cultural discourses such that suicide can be regarded a self-sacrifice by which one assumes for the general good "the role of the surrogate victim" (Girard 23). Historically, women, immigrants, and ethnic minorities have been especially vulnerable to such forms of violence. Religious minorities are vulnerable, too, to silencing in times of crisis including the post-9/11 profiling of Muslims as terrorists.

Because of her gender, race, and religion, the Muslim woman is multiply marked as a victim. She suffers a violent death that polarizes public opinion at least among Reta and her friends. They assume that she is either evil or innocent, though they consider themselves "outside the circle of good and evil" (*Unless* 116). Through self-immolation, perhaps for political reasons, the unknown woman commits suicide in a form of violence that provokes terror because it incites copycat acts. Reta fears suicide as a possible explanation for Norah's disappearance. Sadly, neither Reta nor any friend of hers mourns for the Muslim woman, as Reta grieves for Norah. Instead, they regard the woman as different and distance themselves from her, without questioning the causes of her death. Reta's narrative betrays the scapegoat effect in the way that she and Norah are reconciled at the expense of an innocent third party. This process of denial is unconscious but Reta's misapprehension becomes clear to the reader when she writes:

> But it's all right, Norah. We know now, Norah. You can put this behind you. You are allowed to forget. We'll remember it for you, a memory of a memory, we'll do this gladly.
> *Unless* we ask questions. (315–16; emphasis added)

The word "unless" emphasizes the ambivalence of Shields's text: it is still another indication of the dual-voiced discourse and the double consciousness of the embedded critique. The pronoun "we" that is in the first-person plural suggests, moreover, a collective subject that implicates the reader. Ultimately, a misapprehension of the scapegoat effect is the poison of Reta's narrative, unless the reader raises questions.

Shields makes visible for readers the political interestedness of Reta's journal by employing the double-voicedness and double coding of parody. Shields's text locates Reta within discourses of Western individualism and consumer capitalism that involve the oppression and exploitation of non-Western subjects. At the same time, Shields's text maps what it means to be a woman in a global context, and her achievement is significant for creating disidentifying and collective subject positions. The most important question that Shields's text raises is whether the Muslim woman can be forgotten. The answer is implied: she cannot be forgotten any more than a daughter can be "erased" (23).

Perhaps the most troubling of all in this parody is the fact that the Muslim woman never speaks: indeed, she cannot speak because she is dead. Speaking about or for others poses a dilemma for critics because both stances enact the power relation of subject over object but there is a third option. Bal proposes speaking through the other in a way that "precludes an unmodified return of the subject to the state before speaking" ("Enfolding" 327). The transformative potential of this stance demands further exploration, and Bal posits the temporal fold for evolving artistic and feminist practices: "In spite of the dangers of renewed obliteration, [feminism's] endorsing this wavering point of view fully yields new advantages that can help overcome individualist traps without romanticizing sacrifice or idealizing transcendence" (338). In *Unless*, Shields offers precisely this type of re-presentation, and the fold creates an ethical approach to including the other in a relationship that is connected but separate.

Shields's use of time involves a deliberate narrative fold. By employing repetitive time or repeated events for the immolation scene, Shields tells multiple times what happened only once. Initially, Reta brings up the immolation only in passing as something that she read in a newspaper (41). Twice she alludes to it in the middle of the text in association with Norah (65, 213); once again, she mentions it in a conversation with her friends (117–18). However, it is not until the end, when she learns of Norah's direct involvement, that Reta describes the event not in a few words but in two lengthy paragraphs (314–16). By repeating the event – and changing its context from a passing reference to the novel's very climax – Shields transforms its meaning. Once peripheral to Reta's consciousness, the Muslim woman's death becomes central to her own crisis. As Bal argues, "The fold as a figure (of thought, of matter) insists on surface and materiality. This materialism of the fold entails the involvement of the subject within the material experience ... in a relation that is *correlativist"* ("Enfolding" 337, original emphasis). Shields's narrative enacts a rethinking of the significance of the event, casting it as critical.

Furthermore, the metaphorical distance between the Muslim woman as object and Norah as subject – and by extension Reta – is collapsed by physical touch, not sight. In an attempt to put out the flames that engulf the unnamed woman Norah's fingers sink "into the woman's melting flesh" (315). Norah is burned by the dish rack and plastic bag, the material commodities that she takes home from Honest Ed's department store. This climactic scene portrays an embodied subject that is connected with the other on personal, social, and economic levels. Norah must be lifted away "bodily in a single arc" but the fire scars her hands. By foregrounding the body, Shields's text exceeds a postmodern discourse of the subject: the text becomes a creative and ethical gesture towards a collective subject. Although Norah acts "without thinking" (315), her intervention assumes a connection of the self and other. The red rash on her hands recalls Norah's rash behaviour. Yet Norah's "reckless" act can be seen (58) also as bold and representative of a feminist practice to complement theory. The daughter with a bent head signifies not a lack of worth but a bending of pride; in fact, the root of "worth," which is "wer," means to bend or to turn.[7] The narrative arc traces an allegorical turning, then, from pride and metaphysical selfhood.

Correspondingly, the effect of the climactic event on the reader also changes over the course of the novel from minimal to maximal. There are at least two further effects. The narrative time is slowed down by the repetition of the event, and with the climactic description it comes to a pause that is similar in effect to a close-up, a cinematic technique designed to make an audience think. Like the security video from Honest Ed's that "captured and then saved" the event (315), the narrative bears witness to the violence, and, by stretching time, the narrative pause allows time for a commemoration or ethical "remembrance of the dead" (Bal, "Enfolding" 340). As Bal remarks, the fold becomes a "performance of *attention*" – a "keen and ambivalent attention [that] does not repeat the violence; it counters it" (344; original emphasis).[8] In addition, because there is a delay in presenting the immolation until the end, its significance, far from being forgotten, is heightened. The delay in presenting the cause of Norah's trauma turns the reading process into a *casse-tête*, or narrative puzzle, and an enigma that engages the reader.

Many gaps remain at the close of Reta's narrative despite her discovery of the cause of Norah's trauma. Such gaps have important implications not only for the narrator but also for the reader. Though in her novels, letters, and journal Reta negotiates the discourses of feminism and individualism, she is arrested by a medical diagnosis of Norah's state. Tom believes she suffers from post-traumatic stress disorder but Reta, who is still in denial, stubbornly resists the idea: "The problem is, I'm not sure I believe in the thunderclap of trauma" (269). She maintains that Norah's victimization is related to an identity politics that is solely based on gender differences: "the world is split in two, between those who are handed power at birth ... encoded with a seemingly random chromosome determinate" and those who are not (270). She clings to an identity politics.

The text stages a contest, however, of feminist and scientific discourses. Reta admits that "it may be that I am partly right and partly wrong" and so is Tom (310). Initially Tom appears to be correct about Norah's present crisis, just as he is right to suspect Danielle's past trauma: "her mother had tried to strangle her" at eighteen (316). But the final chapter continues to emphasize the word *unless* as a marker of the relative positions of these discourses. The scientific discourse of the medical profession is a site of struggle for power over "people's bodies, their health, their life and death" (Foucault, "Subject" 420). Neither Reta nor Tom offers a singular truth about Norah's crisis, but both offer interpretations that engage the reader. Shields's parody resists closure and ends with ambivalence. In the end all of Reta's explanatory narratives fail, particularly that of the ironically named Westerman, but Danielle, too, is in the process of rewriting her memoir. Of the three generations of feminist subjects that are represented by Danielle, Reta, and Norah, all are called into question. The discourses of the first two are undermined, at least in part, and the third is silenced.

Reta's autobiographical self-development remains incomplete and provisional because she has not fully confronted the political, economic, and ethical implications of the Muslim woman's immolation. In economic and political contexts, the crisis is unresolved, despite the supposedly happy ending of Norah's return. Implicit in this open ending is a failure of individualist and Western discourses including the return home and the search for identity. The encounter of both mother and daughter with the Muslim woman remains unexplained, revealing the limits of such discourses. Furthermore, the transformative potential of Reta's autobiography goes largely unrealized. Shields's text focuses the reader's attention on the urgent present tense by suspending Reta between the *"already"* of the past and the *"not yet"* of the future (313;original emphasis). This ending creates a torsion of the narrative into ambivalence, as Shields deliberately troubles the autobiographical form and the feminist subject.

The reader's generic expectations of a narrative trajectory towards self-perception and transformation are raised by the confessional and autobiographical discourses, but Shields frustrates these expectations. In fact, Shields's parody implies the reverse: the feminist subject is neither stable nor autonomous. This statement is equally true of Danielle and Norah. In this and other crisis-driven autobiographies, the reader is "shaken out of conventional expectations and becomes implicated in emerging identities and the cultures that they and their crises create" (Egan 228). For this reason, such texts make clear that "the politics of autobiography are more than personal and extend into the desire for change beyond any individual life in question, so explorations of the individual life and death seek communal meaning" (Egan 229). Shields's reader is left with the image of Danielle's hand tracing an "arc in the air" as a political gesture towards change (228). This image becomes the novelist's comment on the ongoing nature of women's life writing and interpretive processes.

A community of women writers is the moral centre of the novel, not the female protagonist. In addition, the text focuses on another community at Promise Hostel that models a "goodness" based on social action. The Anglican community takes in the homeless, offers food and shelter to strangers, does their laundry, and cleans their "messes of urine and vomit" (191–2). Theirs is no mere simulation of an iconic goodness, like the saintly Norah's sign or the feminist Reta's autobiography. Nor is theirs the "easy unthinkingness of people's claim to 'spirituality'" in a consumer culture (185). This religious community's social and ethical practices render Reta and Tom speechless. The Winters' silence, like Norah's, exposes gaps in the dominant discourses, in particular the denial of scapegoating and the need for resistance of collective violence and exclusion. In contrast to Reta's personal and forgotten "religious practice," which resembles her father's lapsed Presbyterianism and her mother's abandoned Catholicism (147), Promise Hostel performs a collective practice of "following Christ's example" by giving to the poor and identifying with the victim and the outcast (191). This identification is derived from a biblical text, which in its "treatment of victimage" takes "the perspective of the victim rather than ... the persecutors" (Girard 18). The active community in its dynamic practice also differs from static saints who inspire a fear or passivity that might arouse violence. As Reta admits, "Virtue is performance" (223). In her crisis, her writing moves towards an ethical approach, rather like Shields's own practice.

The self-reflexive narrative strategies that Shields uses in her novel's meta-autobiography – embedding the narrating self in culture, presenting a crisis to decentre the subject, and foregrounding the processes of identity construction – distance the reader from Reta in order to rethink the subject of feminism. On every level Shields's narrative provokes thought about interconnected and collective subjects. Her text brings to mind a comment of Nicole Brossard, a writer who also employs self-reflexive narrative strategies, such as parody, intertextuality, use of a foreign language, and the creation of representative female characters and their stories. Brossard urges women to think of themselves as writer-critics and their writing as feminist critique (229).[9] In *Unless*, Shields proves to be precisely this kind of writer-critic. The self-representation of Reta within the parodic frame is more subtle, complex, and political than critics might think. Shields's narrative exceeds not only feminist and postmodernist discourses, but also theoretical discourses, perhaps even those of Rosemary Hennessy or Judith Butler.

Shields's critique incorporates not only a spatial dimension, as suggested by a multiplicity of meanings, but also a temporal dimension, which includes a sense of history, as suggested by an unfolding of interconnected events. Throughout her career Shields's consistent experimentation with temporality and non-linearity is purposeful. In particular, she uses the narrative fold to create "a fiction that form[s] a sort of pocket for its own exegesis" ("Arriving" 246); she thereby seeks to embody "an inquiry into language held in an envelope of language" (251). Having experimented with the narrative fold, she makes a conscious claim for literary artists and women writers as historical agents of change: "We need serious critical analysis, of course, but not the throttling sort of theorizing that ... places limits on fiction's possibilities ("Arriving" 247). The critique of the writer-critic can surpass the theorist's in a capacity to suggest new possibilities of political and social transformation. Simply put, the artist's text creates a gesture towards change that exceeds the theorist's.

In *Unless*, Shields returns to her experimentation with autobiography and the mise en abyme to interrogate the subject of feminism, as represented by author and translator Reta Winters. For this purpose, Shields foregrounds the contradictory discourses of truth and identity that construct the subject of autobiography. Furthermore, the parodic frame that distances the reader from Reta's limited perspective, and the embedded crisis that draws attention to the urgent present, create a mirroring encounter between the narrator and reader. These representations, which occur at the level of the implied author and not the narrator-protagonist, raise unsettling questions. Can the feminist discourse of Reta or Danielle be passed on to the next generation that is represented by Norah? Are contemporary feminisms so immersed in Western discourses as to be dead? Shields herself is a woman who writes self-consciously at the turn of the millennium when postmodern and feminist critiques of the subject converge. The self-reflexivity of the text indicates that Shields's political project is to critique the subject of feminism by making it an object of inquiry. She takes aim at autobiographical discourses that reiterate Western ideologies of individualism and autonomous selfhood. By re-presenting these ideologies and the subjects that they construct, *Unless* serves a parodic function in revealing the limits of these dominant discourses. Shields uses a crisis to destabilize the subject, to draw attention to the discursive subject, and, most importantly, to expose the political and ethical realities from which a postmodern concept of an entirely theoretical subject remains aloof. Shields problematizes her subject's relationship to language by showing Reta's contradictory positions in contesting discourses. Just as Norah loses her speech, Reta's explanatory narratives fail, particularly a second-wave identity politics. Nevertheless, the text reaffirms Danielle's insistence upon the transformative potential of dynamic and evolving feminist practices.

Ultimately, Shields employs both postmodernist and feminist approaches in order to critique the subject of feminism as a particular, historical construct, and she does so at a moment when it is no longer possible to assume a universal subject of feminism or to ignore the exclusion of non-Western women. As Hennessy contends, "The task of writing history from a materialist feminist standpoint is to labor continually to release that 'other,' the unsaid of feminist praxis, and through this process of ongoing critique, strengthen the oppositional power of feminism's collective subject and emancipatory aims" (138). The spectre of the Muslim woman troubles Reta's narrative just as it troubles Norah's memory. By analogy, the figure points to Shields's historical predicament of straddling distinct but separate waves of feminism. In a post-9/11 context, it is a spectre of a future in which gendered or racialized subjects, young or old, are at risk of further silencing. The historical context creates, in effect, a heightened sense of urgency for the reader. The figure of the Muslim woman unveils, finally, the sacrificial logic or collective violence that is encoded in the discursive, socio-economic, and political systems that construct Reta's identities as a white, Western, and liberal feminist. These are the very systems in which Reta, and by extension the reader, are shown to be implicated. *Unless* is purposefully designed as a narrative enigma to present the reader with an opportunity to rethink the subject of feminism, to re-examine discourses of self-representation, and to rediscover feminism's liberating possibilities. Shields's work offers a trapdoor by which new, global, collective subjects of the third wave can escape "the vanity trap" of individualism and make meaningful connections in solidarity with others.

Conclusion

Through the narrative art of a creative writer, Carol Shields makes concrete for readers the abstract ideas of literary theory in relation to women's lives. By blending theory with representations of women's lives, especially her characters' self-writing, Shields makes visible and subverts cultural assumptions about autobiography, the author, the body, the self, and the changing subject of feminism. She questions dominant discourses, such as masculine selfhood and Western individualism, implicating in them even white middle-class feminists who are, ironically, among the largest segment of her readers. These are the problems written large in her texts, and they have attracted wide readership and won literary awards both nationally and internationally. American-born and one of the most successful Canadian writers of her time, it is no coincidence that she was the first writer ever to win both the Pulitzer Prize and the Governor General's Award for Fiction. Her highly theoretical novels are deceptively simple, accounting for the continuing debates about her critical reception. While her texts perform a postmodern questioning, they do so with a political purpose. By re-examining the major works that represent her entire career, we see a sustained, feminist critique of literary history and critical theory. With a wry and self-conscious voice, Shields breaks with theory, by using theory, even as she moves towards an ethical criticism that raises broad, theoretical, and social questions without prescribing answers. However, she has not always received full credit for this achievement.

Throughout her career as a novelist, Carol Shields sees the novel's ability to perform the tasks of theory without adopting all of its methods. She uses embedded commentaries and portrayals of women writers in complex and metafictional narratives. Her intent to model women's activism in a supposedly post-feminist age is supported by her interviews, essays, and archives. Six novels focus on a woman writer to produce resistant readings of autobiographical discourses, gender stereotypes, and critical theory. Together these examples of autobiographical and fictional writing show us a virtuoso performance of a feminist critique, undermining the politics of who writes and who reads, assumptions that often escape notice. Rereadings of these novels reveal her resistance to Philippe Lejeune's idea of the autobiographical pact, Michel Foucault's understanding of the death of the author, and Jean Baudrillard's notion of simulation. Shields also resists broad categories, such as historical writing and the autonomous self or a universal subject of feminism. Near the end of her career Shields told an American critic, "Teaching has, of course, made me more self-conscious about the act of writing, especially postmodern theories about writing – which I find fascinating but not very useful" (Shields, qtd. in Hollenberg 345). Though often unrecognized, her disruptive strategies and resistance of critical theory are consistently at work in her best-known novels.

In each case, Shields's formal experimentation is a practice that reads against the grain of autobiographical and critical discourses. In *Small Ceremonies* and *The Box Garden*, Judith Gill and Charleen Forrest, a biographer and a poet, respectively, use and resist autobiographical modes in their journals. In *The Republic of Love*, Fay McLeod, a curator and critic, first embraces and then rejects literary and popular romances, and her life informs her writing as she moves towards an ethical criticism. *The Stone Diaries* resists autobiography and historiography by embedding Daisy Goodwill's diaries, letters, and family tree in an apocryphal journal that is Judith Downing's history of her grandmother's life. This text anticipates and frustrates readings of Daisy as a unified autobiographical subject, on the one hand, or a decentred postmodern subject, on the other hand. Finally, the meta-autobiography of *Unless* deconstructs the embedded journal of feminist Reta Winters, turning the subject of feminism into an object of inquiry, while gesturing towards global and collective subjects. Over time, Shields develops complex narrative strategies that incorporate irony, parody, intertextuality, and women's self-representation, with an increasing self-reflexivity and sophistication. By engaging in a long-term project of cultural critique, Shields herself becomes a writer-critic, and her work develops an exemplary practice of ficto-criticism. In effect, she rethinks a feminist critique in a body of work that spans cultural shifts from second-wave feminism to third-wave feminisms, and from critical theory to political and ethical practices.

In the narrative act, Shields stages an inquiry into language and culture while establishing a lively communication with the reader. This interaction becomes a model that relies more on readers than on critics. The novels employ the mise en abyme of a woman writer who is writing about a woman writer; these narratives are elliptical, double, and enigmatic. Shields creates the open-endedness of a narrative fold or spiral not only in the later novels, but also in the double strategies of the early novels: for instance, *Small Ceremonies* and *The Box Garden* were republished together in a single edition as *Duet* (2003). The narrative fold engages the reader in an interpretive act that is provisional and dynamic. As Shields asserts in an early interview, "Language has been important to me from the beginning ... What I have learned, though, in my later books is that I can trust the reader, that I can step off in mid-air, so to speak, and take the reader along. That I don't need to tie up all the ends quite so neatly" (Shields, qtd. in De Roo 48). While focusing on writing and reading processes, Shields explores multiple perspectives, the mystery of the other, and the possibilities of fiction.

Carol Shields focuses on the reading process by designing for the reader a puzzle or game and a "partnership of creativity" (Shields, qtd. in Anderson 150). Her overarching concerns are the reception of women's lives and the politics of self-representation. As she states in an interview with Canadian journalist Eleanor Wachtel, "I see books demeaned because they deal with the material of women's lives" ("Interview" 26). Instead, she celebrates women's community, interaction, and agency especially in the form of cultural commentary: "Have you ever noticed when women tell stories there's a lot of what looks like unnecessary detail?" ("Interview" 41). She examines the same concerns in her early criticism of Susanna Moodie, just as she does in a relatively recent biography of Jane Austen that is also written against the grain of generic conventions. As a writer-critic, Shields takes a historical view of an ongoing tradition of women's life writing that includes the novel, which she calls "the only literary form in which women have participated from its very beginning" (Shields, qtd. in Anderson 147). This tradition is already "about three hundred years old" (Shields, qtd. in Maharaj 11). Still, its political urgency continues into the present.

Shields uses the novel's multiple voices to depict diverse representations of intersubjectivity and community. Simultaneously, she uses autobiographical discourses to subvert the autonomous male self of literary autobiography and to reinscribe a feminist critique of Western individualism. In a political project that is sustained over an entire career, Shields embraces "the idea of playing with language to make a point" (Shields, qtd. in Wachtel, "Interview" 44). While depicting women's writing, she interrogates history – "what it is, who gets to write it, and what it's for" (Shields, qtd. in Hollenberg 341). For this reason, she deliberately crosses the line between fiction and non-fiction. Her early novels clearly display more political edge than critics might think. Later in her career, *The Stone Diaries* draws international awards and far-reaching literary criticism. Yet this novel, too, must be reread as neither autobiography nor historiography – neither strictly first-person nor third-person narration – but a hybrid of women's life writing and social commentary in the form of a feminist critique. This reading also informs rereadings of *Swann*, *The Republic of Love*, and *Unless* in a reassessment of Shields's body of work that is long overdue.

Through an emphasis on Carol Shields as a writer-critic, it is possible to address some of the deficiencies in the criticism and reception of her oeuvre. Two critical problems, in particular, are a frequent failure to look beyond the focus on women's lives, and a common misconception that Shields changes narrative strategies in mid-career. Despite some positive responses in recent appraisals, critics have not always given Shields sufficient credit.[1] In 1988, as Shields notes in her interview with Harvey De Roo in *West Coast Review*, "The praise for my recent books [*Swann* and *Various Miracles*] has indeed been offset by a certain amount of casual disparagement of my earlier novels" (47). She argues that the books are undervalued due to their focus on the lives of women, regardless of their subtle complexity and embedded commentary. She points to a subversive interest in multiple perspectives in *The Republic of Love* and an interest in "hidden perspectives," even "writing from a void, completely masking the narrator, but I haven't managed it yet." She would do so in *The Stone Diaries*. Her satirical aim is to "set up a story traditionally ... then turn it upside down or take it into another reality" (Shields, qtd. in De Roo 48–9). Carol Shields focuses on the language of ordinary life in order to show that it can be either freeing or constraining. She has a remarkably coherent vision of her purpose and narrative strategies from the outset of her career. Any confusion about the early novels in opposition to the late ones belongs to the critics who, like De Roo, label them domestic novels in spite of their formal experiments and political purpose. He assumes that both begin with *Swann*. By 2008, the author of the first book-length study on Shields, Alex Ramon, remarks that "her work anticipates current re-evaluations of postmodernist thought by over twenty years" (178). Consistent genre mixing and feminist critique are indeed apparent in her highly theoretical novels. An appropriation of Shields to a postmodernist agenda would nevertheless be repeated throughout her career.

At times Shields is lost in the shifting grounds between realism and postmodernism. Many associate her with a postmodern playfulness. Edward Eden rightly argues that Shields's experimentation is "more than simply a language game" because her metafiction demonstrates the limits and possibilities of life writing (9–10). Yet Eden claims, too, that with *Swann* there is a decisive turn in Shields's career.

Likewise, other summaries of her career are divided into the early novels and the late novels. For example, *The Concise Oxford Companion to Canadian Literature* (2001) groups together the first four novels, with all being labelled domestic novels and *Small Ceremonies* being "the best and most consistently believable" (442–3). Only subsequent works are lauded for an attention to detail and ordinary people despite some coincidences. The entry expands an earlier one by Constance Rooke that predated *Swann*. One comment that is conspicuous by its absence from the recent entry involves Rooke's reservation about Shields's embedded commentary and a "tendency of [her] characters to meditate upon or debate the nature of biography, fiction, or history in a way that is sometimes obtrusive" (752). By contrast, Lorraine York later writes approvingly of Shields's focus on a "fading belief in historiographic detachment" ("Shields" 1038). Ahead of her critics, in 1987, Shields remarks on history and objectivity, "I like to think that these categories ... are breaking down as rapidly as the boundaries between genres, and that this process has been accelerated by feminist writing" (Shields, qtd. in De Roo 39). York's summary in the *Encyclopedia of Literature in Canada* (2002) again separates the late works from early ones, and the early novels get scant attention while later ones get a lot of ink.

York revises her opinion, however, in a more recent study of Shields's literary celebrity. She praises Shields's wry voice despite her apparent modesty:

> I had ... seen her as quietly acquiescing in the media's depiction of her as an unassuming, middle-class, heterosexual woman with an allegiance to domestic interests ... But then *Unless* appeared and changed my perspective ... for at the end of her career, Shields summoned up the willingness – and the requisite anger – to set the record straight. (*Celebrity* 165–6)

While York is correct in identifying the satiric voice and its continuity over Shields's career (159), she implies that Shields's voice changed near the end of her career. It is in fact the critic, not the novelist, who changes her tone. Shields's consistency is undeniable, in contrast to changing critical tastes.

Despite her subtle feminist critique, Shields is caught between the shifting grounds of not only realism and postmodernism but also second-wave and third-wave feminisms. An entry on Shields in *Contemporary Canadian Authors* (1996) gives another mixed reception by damning her with faint praise: "Reviewers argue about whether or not Shields's focus on womanhood represents a feminist viewpoint, but most critics believe that it does not" (418–19). By stressing that *Swann*'s Sarah Maloney chooses motherhood over activism, this entry alludes to Laura Groening's article of 1991 in the *Canadian Forum*. "Still in the Kitchen: The Art of Carol Shields" denounces Shields's feminist character who "becomes pregnant at the end of the novel and immediately rejects her earlier political commitment" (17). Lisa Sims Brandon equally condemns homemaker Daisy Goodwill as anti-feminist. By taking a historical view of the novelist's entire career one can see Shields's precarious position in the schisms of critical debate.

In retrospect, such negative criticism appears retrograde for its second-wave feminist reaction to a progressive cultural critique. Conversely, the attention of Wachtel is favourable. In 1989, she edited a special issue devoted to Shields in *Room of One's Own: A Feminist Journal of Literature and Criticism*. Her introduction admits the flippancy of Maloney and domesticity of characters in the early novels but recognizes Shields's critical neglect. While setting the parameters for feminist analyses, Wachtel echoes De Roo to a degree:

"Four years ago, Shields started to publish work that was different from what she'd written before. It was more whimsical, more non-naturalistic, what used to be called 'experimental,' but now passes as 'post-modern'" ("Introduction" 3). At the same time, Wachtel sees that Shields's career straddles critical theory and political practices, precariously, and yet successfully. She understands Shields's project as postmodern *and* feminist. In an accompanying interview, Shields confesses a feminist perspective that came from Betty Friedan's *The Feminine Mystique* and her speech in Ottawa during the 1970s ("Interview" 26). But in a follow-up letter she takes an ambivalent position: "Your question of when exactly I became a feminist ... puzzled me, and I've more or less decided I've always been" ("Introduction" 3). This ambivalence is misread by other critics who fail to see Shields as a bridging figure between second-wave feminism and third-wave feminist theory and practice.

Shields remains ambivalent in later interviews. In 1998, when Donna Krolik Hollenberg calls *Swann* a satire on academics and feminist critics, Shields argues that it both satirizes and praises them (345). In another conversation with Marjorie Anderson, Shields distances herself from second-wave feminists by insisting, "I would like to see more novels about intelligent women, instead of novels about women as victims" (147). Her interviews and oeuvre register a cultural shift towards third-wave practices. It is because of this shift, as Misha Kavka remarks elsewhere, that a universalizing tendency or "clarity about the object, goal, and even definition of feminism now seems no longer possible or even desirable"; instead, provisional and ongoing feminist projects are best regarded as "a set of practices without a single definition" (x–xi). Kavka locates the shift between the late 1970s and the early 1990s (ix), the period when Shields wrote most of her novels. In this historical context, Shields must be seen as participating in and, to some extent, leading the emerging theoretical and feminist discourses. Kavka's outline is illuminating in this regard:

> We also mark our own historical positioning and theoretical bias by not assuming feminism to be something that can be adequately captured by a range of representative voices (i.e., the "whole" of feminism would be illuminated if only enough different positions could be included) or by a confessional mode of writing (i.e., "real" feminism would be illuminated by bringing to light marginalized

or silenced voices) or even by a materialist approach that takes the "real" situation into account (i.e., feminism is first and last about the conditions of women's lives). Being in (feminist) history means that these notions of representation, self-identity, and lived experience have been subject to criticism, and this criticism has left its indelible mark on the possible further projects of feminism itself. (xvii)

All of these strategies – multiple voices, autobiographical and confessional modes, emphases on political and social intervention – are everywhere apparent in Shields's oeuvre. While Shields's initial ambivalence is understandable in the context of the social change that was then occurring, it has nonetheless affected the reception of her work, sometimes negatively by dividing her critics. For this reason, corrective readings and re-evaluations of her work are now required.

Because of Carol Shields's resistance to critics, including feminists, we must be sceptical of her reception in comparison with other writers, especially those in the same period who were consecrated by literary critics. In national and international contexts more work must be done on Shields's reception in relation to Michael Ondaatje, for instance. Lorraine York, Marta Dvorak, and Gillian Roberts do some of this important work.[2] *The Stone Diaries* was at times misread while Ondaatje's works were lauded for similar strategies: multiple perspectives, self-reflexivity, mixed genres, and parodies of autobiographical and historical discourses. In addition to Ondaatje, others to whom she can be compared are Rohinton Mistry, Alice Munro, and Margaret Atwood. Dvorak suggests further comparisons to women writers who combine metafiction and life writing in Quebec. Roberts confirms that international awards such as the Pulitzer Prize raised Shields's profile within Canada.

In debates of the same period, Susanna Egan and Gabriele Helms note the expanding genres of autobiography and the timeliness of combined generic and theoretical considerations. Certainly, Carol Shields can be identified with Canadian and international trends towards autobiography studies and ficto-criticism. Sidonie Smith and Julia Watson observe that the autobiographical voice in both creative and critical writing appears widespread and emergent in work as diverse as Herman Rapaport's use of personal criticism and bell hooks's practice of autocritique. Similarly, Aram Veeser's essay collection, *Confessions of the Critics: North American Critics'*

Autobiographical Moves (1996), marks a critical turn to autobiographical modes in the 1990s. Writing practices that combine critical and fictive language, mainly in postmodern and feminist approaches, continue to spread.

Canadian art critic Jeanne Randolph coined the term "ficto-criticism" to describe her own blend of art criticism and art writing, which she developed in response to the Queen Street West art scene in Toronto from the 1970s to the 1990s (231). Informed by feminist and psychoanalytic theories, she consciously emphasized the relationship between subjectivity and objectivity as well as the collaboration between artist and critic.[3] Literary critic Garry Sherbert comments on Randolph's writing: "The cultural significance of ficto-criticism becomes greatly extended when the capacity of art to embody, and thereby collectively share, our subjective experiences and creativity in some external object is generalized" (15). Randolph's criticism moves in the direction of fiction at the same time that Shields's fiction moves in the direction of criticism. Both share a common purpose: to raise critical consciousness while celebrating the subjectivity, not the objectivity, of the writer-critic.

Comparable writing practices that are at once creative and critical have also sprung up in Australia. As in Canada, these practices engage readers with political and ethical concerns and cross genres and genders. In her introduction to a collection of ficto-criticism, Australian critic Amanda Nettelbeck discovers a wide range of writing practices that are influenced by critical theorists, such as Frederic Jameson, Roland Barthes, and Hélène Cixous, as well as contemporary writers, such as Stephen Muecke. The latter offers a deformation of literature in a world of increasingly transnational relations and politics; he promotes writing accompanied by mises en abyme and literary performances of an attraction and entrapment of readers, which he compares to the function of a pitcher plant. The metaphor recalls Shields, who, in *The Stone Diaries*, uses the lady's slipper as an emblem for the reader-trap from which there is no easy exit. Nettelbeck recalls that while ficto-criticism coincides with postmodernism its function is primarily ethical. She insists that it escapes definition and categories, generating a multiplicity of meanings for readers.

Shields's work itself generates a ficto-critical response in the writing of Canadian author Aritha Van Herk. In her ficto-commentary, "Extrapolations from Miracles: Out of Carol Shields," Van Herk reimagines characters from Shields's short story collection entitled

Various Miracles. The characters, who are gathered from many stories, converse in a large feather bed and later on a stalled bus. Van Herk admits, in a footnote, to having "taken advantage of, referred to, and quoted from" Shields's work in her stream-of-consciousness tale (54). The purpose of such "ficto-crypticism" is to pay homage to Shields, who is finally described as "wearing a buttercup yellow dress" and holding in her hand a "wordnet." Van Herk exclaims, "The real miracle is that there are miracles. And Carol Shields stories this wonder." In the companion essays of *In Visible Ink*, Van Herk casts doubt on generic distinctions in a fictional quest for the "degenred book," a goal that she thinks is signalled by Shields's writing. In a war between writer and critic Shields offers the possibility of a hybrid form. However, in pushing the boundaries to excess, Van Herk reveals, by contrast, the subtlety of Shields's work, which refrains from attempting to subvert all conventions. She does not always break boundaries, but bends them to her purpose of seeking an ethical criticism. Shields's language inspires and connects others: in fact, a collection of responses in Van Herk's *Evocation and Echo* shows that the dialogue with Shields is far from over.

In these shifting historical, national, and international contexts, Shields's writing stands out as a model. She anticipates and participates in the autobiographical turn in criticism globally. Shields's career as a novelist offers a model par excellence of a sustained critique of critical, generic, and cultural thought especially among women writers. As a writer-critic, Shields uses complex metafictional strategies, such as the mise en abyme, and autobiographical discourses to frame her work as a cultural artefact. Carol Shields's critical sophistication never comes at the expense of her readers, and she shows them the utmost respect by allowing them to find their own way into the labyrinth that is her work's timely cultural and feminist critique.

Notes

Introduction

1 Brossard coins the term "syncrones" for women writers who synchronize the act of writing and literary criticism. Her words may be translated as follows: women synchronizers, those who are at once writers and critics.

2 See Neil Besner, Alex Ramon, and Marta Dvorak and Manina Jones, and interviews with Shields by De Roo (1988) and Wachtel (1989). See also Conclusion, n1.

3 For more discussion of the social contract, see Lejeune's expanded definition of the autobiographical pact ("Pact" 11–13).

4 Because I am interested in a body of work in novel form that depicts the self-representation of women writers, I leave aside Shields's poetry, drama, and short fiction for others to analyse.

1. The Problem of the Genre

1 For a discussion of life writing as a spectrum of genres that includes self-reflexive metafiction, see Marlene Kadar (*Essays* 10–12); in its relation to Shields, see also Coral Ann Howells (91), Conny Steenman-Marcusse (111), and Chiara Briganti (176).

2 This shortcoming is one that Lejeune acknowledges ("Bis" 131). For a discussion and working definition of autobiography as "discourses of self-representation" (*Autobiographics* 3), see Gilmore's article "The Mark of Autobiography: Postmodernism, Autobiography, and Genre." As Quebec novelist Nicole Brossard insists, too, "In reality there is no fiction" (*Lovhers* 15).

3 Susan Billingham observes that the novel is "full of writers: novelists, biographers, and scholars" (277). See also Sarah Gamble (41), Malcolm Page (175), and Alex Ramon (14). Bruce MacDonald (149) and Faye Hammill draw parallels between the American-born Shields and Furlong Eberhardt ("Native" 97). While many critics note the mise en abyme, none sees Shields's use of this self-reflexive technique as a feminist critique of the autobiographical pact.

4 Carol Shields, *Small Ceremonies* (Toronto: Vintage, [1976] 1995), 37. All further references are to this edition. All references to *The Box Garden* are to: *The Box Garden* (Toronto: Vintage, [1977] 1990).

5 Here I think of Shields as the "implied author," a persona that Wallace Martin distinguishes from "the person who did the writing" (135); in contrast, the "real author" is simply unavailable in the text (Prince 42).

6 I borrow the term "mirror text" from Mieke Bal (*Narratology* 146).

7 *Carol Shields Fonds*, 1954–98, Literary Manuscripts Collection, Ottawa: Library and Archives Canada, 1994, 1997, LMS-0212 1994–13 69. This and subsequent quotations from archival manuscripts come from the *Carol Shields Fonds* in the Literary Manuscripts Collection of Library and Archives Canada in Ottawa. They are identified in parenthetical citations by control, accession, and box number, and when available, file and page number. I wish to thank Catherine Hobbs, Literary Archivist (English language), Canadian Archives and Special Collections, as well as Lynn Lafontaine and Janet Murray for their assistance, and especially Don Shields for permission to quote the manuscripts.

8 Regarding her own poetry, Shields cites Philip Larkin as an influence while modern poetry like Eliot's "disappointed me" (Shields, qtd. in Wachtel, "Interview" 21).

9 Eugene Stelzig makes this distinction between fictional autobiography and confession (31).

10 Hutcheon views Shields's work as metafiction and Billingham uses "self-conscious realism" for Shields's genre mixing (276), as though it were intended to straddle the line between modernism and postmodernism.

11 Still, Charleen is the "runaway younger sister" who eloped suddenly (78), like Lydia in *Pride and Prejudice*.

12 Lanser also notes that works such as anthologies that are organized to show difference and ethnic or racial identities would not proliferate until the 1980s (262).

2. The Problem of the Author

1 *Carol Shields Fonds*, LMS-0212 1994–13 33, file 7. It is important to
  recall that Shields's essay "Arriving Late: Starting Over" reveals her
  intent to make fiction "an inquiry into language held in an envelope of
  language" (251), an intent that is also demonstrated in a concrete way
  by her archive. The business card identifies author Edward O. Phillips,
  187 Grosvenor Avenue, Westmount, Quebec, H3Y 2S5 (with this added
  correction: "425 Wood Avenue"). He writes on the recto side, "Carol – I
  was enjoying the book so much I rationed myself – no more than half a
  chapter a day. I truly hated to finish." He adds on the verso side, "The
  Double Hook, our Canadian bookstore, says the novel has been selling
  really well. I had to order a copy and wait for the next shipment."
2 An earlier version of this essay was presented at the Canadian
  Literature Symposium, "The Worlds of Carol Shields," at the University
  of Ottawa on 28 April 2012. A fellow presenter, Cynthia Sugars, finds
  resemblances in Swann to Lowther and Sarah Binks with implications
  for both gender and nation (81–2).
3 It is important to recall that Frederic Jameson calls "pastiche" mimicry
  without laughter or "parody that has lost its sense of humor" because
  the intent is serious ("Postmodernism" 114) For this reason, Heidi
  Hansson compares *Swann* to A.S. Byatt's *Possession* (355); Susan Grove
  Hall (46), Susan Elizabeth Sweeney (23), and Burkhard Niederhoff (71)
  also view *Swann* as parodic.
4 See Brian Johnson's essay "Necessary Illusions: Foucault's Author
  Function in Carol Shields's *Swann*." See also Helen Buss, Clara Thomas,
  Mary Eagleton, Kathy Barbour, and Sarah Gamble's articles on *Swann*.
5 Carol Shields, *Swann* (New York: Random House [1987], 1995), 180. All
  further references are to this edition.
6 Jean Baudrillard defines the hyperreal as the vicious circle of "a political
  space" that is "characterised by a *precession of the model*" ([*sic.*] 32, 35–6;
  original emphasis). See chapter 4's discussion of Daisy's image as a tragic
  heroine, for "wherever she goes, her story marches ahead of her" (122).
7 Shields also draws on real authors, Kent Thompson and Frederick
  Philip Grove, to satirize the naturalized Canadian in *Small Ceremonies*
  (Thompson 76, Spettigue 324). Faye Hammill discusses Shields further
  in relation to Canadian nationalism ("Circles" 118–19).
8 Shields signals the same problem in *Unless*, when novelist Reta Winters
  has the dubious honour of winning the "Offenden Prize" (81). Hers

resembles the Orange Prize, an international award for the best novel written in English by a woman – an award that Shields won for *Larry's Party* in 1997. With characteristic irony Shields dubs her protagonist Xeta d'Orange (249).

9 Swann's "disappearance" at the conference evokes Lowther's sudden disappearance days before a conference of the League of Canadian Poets in Victoria, where Lowther was to be the chair in September 1975. Her last collection of poetry, *A Stone Diary*, had been accepted for publication by Oxford University Press and it was printed in 1977 (a reprint is forthcoming).

3. The Problem of the Body

1 Carol Shields, *The Republic of Love* (Toronto: Vintage, [1992] 1994), 319. All further references are to this edition.
2 The word "courtship" is later italicized (LMS-0212 1994–13 38, f. 3, p. 26), and the intent is clearly allegorical.
3 Lorraine McMullen notes that the title was, however, already taken (46).
4 Even Shields's editor, Mindy Werner, remarks on the manuscript, "I *love* this!!" (LMS-0212 1994–13 38, f. 4, p. 340).
5 Critics stress Shields's emphasis on chance or coincidence (Clara Thomas, "Swerves" 153; Irvine 142; Tuhkunen 112; Groening 17; Vauthier, "Miracles" 191), but her emphasis must be understood as parodic and exaggerated to make visible the gaps in dominant discourses that make chance an unquestioned cause of events, rendering social causes invisible.

4. The Problem of the Subject

1 For example, see David Williams's "Making Stories, Making Selves: 'Alternate Versions' in *The Stone Diaries*" (*Canadian Literature* 186 [2005]: 10–28), 15, and Simone Vauthier's "Ruptures in Carol Shields's *The Stone Diaries*," 185. An earlier version of this essay was published in *Studies in Canadian Literature* 35.1 (2010): 127–46.
2 All references to *The Stone Diaries* are to the first edition (Toronto: Random House, 1993).
3 See chapter 1n1.
4 No date for this draft is given; it is simply marked "very early." An early name for Daisy Flett is Elinor Harris, as Alex Ramon also notes (131).

I agree with Ramon that Shields writes against the grain of autobiography and historiography (129), and that she unsettles the balance between Daisy's voice and other voices in the text (132–3), but I cannot equate Daisy's voice with the narrative voice, even if her voice is regarded as both inside and outside the narrated events.

5 See *Carol Shields Fonds*, LMS-0212 1994–13 43. Literary archivist Catherine Hobbs confirms that the corrections are in the hand of editor Hazel Coleman. This wording does not appear in earlier drafts; for instance, compare the draft dated August 1992 (LMS-0212 1994–13 41, f. 14, pp. 22, 329), in which the passage reads as follows: "(Does Grandma Flett actually say this last aloud? I'm not sure. I've lost track of what's real and what isn't)."

6 In fact, Potter is named by Alex Clark, in the *Guardian* (London, England), as being responsible for ensuring Shields's reputation internationally when he "happened upon Shields's fifth novel, *Swann*, and promptly snapped it up – together with its author's backlist" (*Guardian*, 18 July 2003, 23).

7 Compare the early wording, "I'm still here – inside the tiny (powdery splintery) bones and slack flesh, the sockets of eyes, shoulder, hip, teeth. I'm here" (LMS-0212 1994–13 40, f. 1).

8 No date is given for the corrected copy.

9 This earlier version of the poem is comparable to one that is dated 31 December 1992 (LMS-0212 1994–13 42, f. 6).

10 In contrast to Alice, a second-wave feminist, Judith does not come of age until the third wave of feminism in the late 1980s and early 1990s. At the age of thirty, when this life narrative is published in 1993, Judith has undertaken a feminist revisionist project of recovering Daisy's personal history, as the epigraph suggests.

11 Though Alice is at the time unaware of her letter (237), Daisy, like Clarentine, starts a new life by secretly writing a letter. Shields makes the same observation about Susanna Moodie in *Small Ceremonies* (102); again, she blurs the line between fact and fiction.

12 The photo is dated 10 October 1935 and marked "Donald Hugh Shields, almost a year old." After examining photos of family and friends in the archive (LMS-0212 1994–13, boxes 45, 67, and 79), I believe that Judith Downing, Jilly Taylor, and Sophie Flett-Roy may be identified as Meg Shields, Beth Taylor as Catherine Shields, Lissa Taylor as Sara Shields, and Hugh Flett-Roy as John Shields. I thank Anne Giardini, Shields's eldest daughter, for identifying herself in the photos of Alice Downing and Rain Taylor, and I thank Anne and Meg for identifying their sisters'

photos. Carol Shields stated that all of her daughters are in the album, as was her family's home in Ottawa at 583 The Driveway (Shields, qtd. in Joan Thomas 59). For more on photos, see also Deborah Schnitzer and Catherine Hobbs.

13 See *Carol Shields Fonds*, LMS-0212 1997–04 54, f. 4. Inez Warner's diary (annotated by Carol Shields) is dated 6 May–12 June 1969 (see pp. 3, 12, 34, 45, and 61). *Small Ceremonies* is dedicated to Shields's mother.

14 There are two photos of Louise Wyatt (LMS-0212 1994–13 67, f. 21), a columnist for the *London Free Press* and correspondent of Shields, who was of the same generation as her mother.

15 Shields and Howard also co-wrote *A Celibate Season* (1991).

16 For example, see *Carol Shields Fonds*, LMS-0212 1994–13 41, f. 24, p. 43 or f. 25, p. 23.

17 "Ha" also appears beside descriptions of Alice's failed novel in "Illness and Decline" (LMS-0212 1994–13 41, f. 28, p. 18), and Pinky Fulham's flattening by a vending machine in "Work" (LMS-0212 1994–13 41, f. 26, p. 24). These comments may be Meg's or Catherine's, according to archivist Catherine Hobbs (in personal correspondence to the author, 26 July 2012).

5. The Problem of the Subject of Feminism

1 An earlier version of this essay was presented to the Association of Canadian College and University Teachers of English at the Canadian Congress of Social Sciences and Humanities at Concordia University in Montreal on 31 May 2010. All references to *Unless* are to the first edition (Toronto: Random House, 2002). I borrow the term "crisis-driven autobiography" from Susanna Egan (9, 228).

2 Roy refers to interviewer Eleanor Wachtel, who uses the same label in *Random Illuminations* (Wachtel 18, 157). Shields reportedly calls *Unless* her most overtly feminist book, but only in the sense that it insists women's writing must be taken seriously.

3 For more discussion, see Mary Eagleton ("Matter" 82) and Hilde Staels (120).

4 Shields associates "luck" and "genes" with dominant discourses, just as Jean Baudrillard associates "accident" with a convergence of "genetic and verbal codes" (105–7). Laura Groening wrongly assumes that Shields believes "most strongly in luck and genes" and "has no use for instruments of social change" such as feminism (17).

5 For a succinct discussion of second- and third-wave feminism, see Misha Kavka, ix–xxvi.

6 I think here of Judith Butler's discussion of gender as performative and "mimetic" (186).

7 I refer to the definition of "wer-2" in *The American Heritage Dictionary of the English Language*, 3rd ed. (Boston: Houghton Mifflin, 1992), 2132.

8 Derrida proposes the pocket as a structural metaphor (71), though for somewhat different reasons; for more on the "pharmakos" and "escape from metaphysical desire," see René Girard (50, 78–80).

9 The term "writer-critics" is my translation for Brossard's description of women writers as "syncrones" (227): "les femmes syncrones, celles-ci étant l'écrivaine et la critique qui, au-delà d'une complicité circonstantielle, sont parfaitement syncronisées dans l'espace mental de ce que veut et pense l'écriture" (229).

Conclusion

1 In 2007, Christian Riegel names her one of the most successful Canadian writers of her time (217); and Lorraine York calls her an international star on a par with Margaret Atwood and Michael Ondaatje (*Celebrity* 147). Editors of early essay collections on Shields link this success, in part, to her genre mixing. In 2003, Neil Besner applauds a "unique talent for interweaving the genres of fiction, biography, and autobiography" (9). Also in 2003, Edward Eden praises a critical practice that "implies a bond between reader and writer, world and text" (7). In 2007, Marta Dvorak addresses again the neglect of Shields, especially of her early novels and short stories. Recently a collection edited by David Staines from the 2012 Canadian Literature Symposium has come out; see *The Worlds of Carol Shields* (2014).

2 See Dvorak's introduction in *La Création Biographique* (1997), York's fifth chapter in *Literary Celebrity in Canada* (2007), and Gillian Roberts's third chapter in *Prizing Literature: The Celebration and Circulation of National Culture* (2011). Dvorak compares Shields to Gail Scott and Daphne Marlatt, too.

3 For example, she wrote a parallel text for the installation and artist book of visual artist Joey Morgan (*The Man Who Waits and Sleeps While I Dream* [Regina: MacKenzie Art Gallery, 1999]). Morgan added her prose to Randolph's critical essay and both experimented with autobiographical modes (Randolph 242–3).

Bibliography

Aikins, Mary S. """In Her Own Words." Interview with Carol Shields." *Reader's Digest* Sept. (2003): 64–70.

Anderson, Marjorie. "Interview with Carol Shields." *Prairie Fire* 16.1 (1995): 139–50.

Atwood, Margaret. "Another Night Visit." In *Tributaries: An Anthology*. Ed. Barry Dempster. Oakville: Mosaic, 1978. 60.

– "Last Testaments: Pat Lowther and John Thompson (1978)." In *Second Words: Selected Critical Prose*. Toronto: Anansi, 1982. 307–12.

– "Saturday Review: Lives and Letters: To the Light House." *Guardian* (London, England), 26 July 2003, 28. http://books.guardian.co.uk/departments/generalfiction/story/0,6000,1005905,00.html (accessed 4 Oct. 2005).

Bakhtin, Mikhail. *Problems of Dostoevsky's Poetics*. Translated and edited by Caryl Emerson. Minneapolis: University of Minnesota Press, 1984.

Bal, Mieke. "Enfolding Feminism." In *Feminist Consequences: Theory for the New Century*. Ed. Elisabeth Bronfen and Misha Kavka. New York: Columbia University Press, 2001. 321–2.

– *Narratology: Introduction to the Theory of Narrative*. Translated by Christine van Boheemen. Toronto: University of Toronto Press, 1985.

Barbour, Kathy. "The Swann Who Laid the Golden Egg: A Cautionary Tale of Deconstructionist Cannibalism in *Swann*." In *Carol Shields, Narrative Hunger, and the Possibilities of Fiction*. Ed. Edward Eden and Dee Goertz. Toronto: University of Toronto Press, 2003. 255–82.

Barthes, Roland. "The Death of the Author." In *Modern Criticism and Theory: A Reader*. 1988. Ed. David Lodge. New York: Longman, 1990. 167–72.

Baudrillard, Jean. *Simulations*. Translated by Paul Foss, Paul Patton, and Philip Beitchman. New York: Semiotext(e), 1983.

Beckman-Long, Brenda. "Genre and Gender: Autobiography and Self-Representation in *The Diviners.*" *English Studies in Canada* 30.3 (2004): 89–110.

– "*The Stone Diaries* as an 'Apocryphal Journal.'" *Studies in Canadian Literature* 35.1 (2010): 127–46.

Benjamin, Walter. "The Work of Art in the Age of Mechanical Reproduction." In *Illuminations.* Edited by Hannah Arendt. Translated by Harry Zohn. New York: Schocken, 1968. 217–42.

Besner, Neil K. "Introduction." In *Carol Shields: The Arts of a Writing Life.* Ed. Neil K. Besner. Winnipeg: Prairie Fire Press, 2003. 9–13.

Billingham, Susan E. "Fragile Tissue: The Fiction of Carol Shields." *British Journal of Canadian Studies* 13.2 (1998): 276–87.

Bourdieu, Pierre. *The Field of Cultural Production.* Edited by Randal Johnson. New York: Columbia University Press, 1993.

Brewster, Elizabeth, Mick Burns, Stephen Michael Bersensky, et al. "P.K. Page, and Lorraine Vernon." "Pat Lowther: A Tribute." *Contemporary Verse Two* 2.1 (1976): 15–17.

Briganti, Chiara. "Fat, Nail Clippings, Body Parts, or the Story of Where I Have Been: Carol Shields and Auto/Biography." In *Carol Shields, Narrative Hunger, and the Possibilities of Fiction.* Ed. Edward Eden and Dee Goertz. Toronto: University of Toronto Press, 2003. 175–200.

Brooks, Toby. *Pat Lowther's Continent: Her Life and Work.* Charlottetown: Gynergy, 2000.

Brossard, Nicole. *Lovhers.* 1980. Translated by Barbara Godard. Montreal: Guernica, 1986.

– "Mouvements et stratégies de l'écriture de fiction." In *Gynocritics: Feminist Approaches to Canadian and Quebec Women's Writing.* Ed. Barbara Godard. Toronto: ECW, 1987. 227–30.

Buss, Helen M. "Abducting Mary and Carol: Reading Carol Shields's *Swann* and the Representation of the Writer through Theories of Biographical Recognition." *English Studies in Canada* 23.4 (1997): 427–41.

– *Mapping Our Selves: Canadian Women's Autobiography.* Montreal: McGill-Queen's University Press, 1993.

Butler, Judith. *Gender Trouble: Feminism and the Subversion of Identity.* 1990. New York: Routledge. 1999.

Carol Shields Fonds. 1954–98. Literary Manuscripts Collection. Ottawa: Library and Archives Canada. 1994, 1997.

Clark, Alex. "Carol Shields: Gifted Writer Famed for Her Masterful Depictions of Ordinary Life." *Guardian* (London, England), 18 July 2003, 23.

Cohn, Dorrit. *The Distinction of Fiction.* Baltimore: Johns Hopkins University Press, 1999.

Cooke, Nathalie. "Reading Reflections: The Autobiographical Illusion in *Cat's Eye*." In *Essays on Life Writing: From Genre to Critical Practice*. Ed. Marlene Kadar. Toronto: University of Toronto Press, 1992. 164–70.

Dällenbach, Lucien. *The Mirror in the Text*. 1977. Translated by Jeremy Whiteley and Emma Hughes. Chicago: University of Chicago Press, 1989.

De Man, Paul. "Autobiography as Defacement." 1979. In *The Rhetoric of Romanticism*. New York: Columbia University Press, 1984. 67–82.

De Roo, Harvey. "A Little Like Flying: An Interview with Carol Shields." *West Coast Review* 23.3 (1988): 38–56.

Denoon, Anne. "Playing with Convention." *Books in Canada* 22.9 (1993): 8–12.

Derrida, Jacques. "The Law of Genre." Translated by Avital Ronell. *Critical Inquiry* 7.1 (1980): 55–81. http://dx.doi.org/10.1086/448088.

Donne, John. "Batter My Heart." In *The Literature of Renaissance England*. Ed. John Hollander and Frank Kermode. New York: Oxford University Press, 1973. 552.

Dostoyevsky, Fyodor. *Crime and Punishment*. Translated by Constance Garnett. New York: Random House, 1956.

Dvorak, Marta. "An Aesthetics of the Ordinary in *Dressing Up for the Carnival*."In *Carol Shields: The Arts of a Writing Life*. Ed. Neil K. Besner. Winnipeg: Prairie Fire Press, 2003. 133–44.

– "Introduction." In *La Création Biographique / Biographical Creation*. Rennes: Presses Universitaires de Rennes, 1997. 17–22.

Dvorak, Marta, and Manina Jones, eds. *Carol Shields and the Extra-Ordinary*. Montreal: McGill-Queen's University Press, 2007.

Eagleton, Mary. "Carol Shields and Pierre Bourdieu: Reading *Swann*." *Critique: Studies in Contemporary Fiction* 44.3 (2003): 313–28.

– "What's the Matter? Authors in Carol Shields's Short Fiction." *Canadian Literature* 186 (2005): 70–84.

Edel, Leon. "The Figure under the Carpet." In *Telling Lives: The Biographer's Art*. Ed. Marc Pachter. Washington, DC: New Republic Books, 1979. 16–34.

Eden, Edward. "Introduction."In *Carol Shields, Narrative Hunger, and the Possibilities of Fiction*. Ed. Edward Eden and Dee Goertz. Toronto: University of Toronto Press, 2003. 3–15.

Egan, Susanna. *Mirror Talk: Genres of Crisis in Contemporary Autobiography*. Chapel Hill: University of North Carolina Press, 1999.

Egan, Susanna, and Gabriele Helms. "Auto/biography? Yes. But Canadian?" *Canadian Literature* 172 (2002): 5–16.

Felman, Shoshana. *Writing and Madness*. 1985. Translated by Martha Noel Evans. Palo Alto: Stanford University Press, 2003.

Finlay, Michael. "Slain Vancouver Poet Wrote of Bloody Death." *Vancouver Sun*, 18 Oct. 1975, 16.

Foucault, Michel. "The Subject of Power." In *Art After Modernism: Rethinking Representation*. Edited by Brian Wallis. New York: New Museum of Contemporary Art, 1984. 417–32.

– "What Is an Author?" In *Modern Criticism and Theory: A Reader*. 1988. Edited by David Lodge. New York: Longman, 1990. 197–210.

Fulford, Robert. "The Death-Haunted Poetry of Pat Lowther." *Saturday Night* 92.4 (1977): 71.

Gamble, Sarah. "Filling the Creative Void: Narrative Dilemmas in *Small Ceremonies*, the *Happenstance* Novels, and *Swann*." In *Carol Shields, Narrative Hunger, and the Possibilities of Fiction*. Ed. Edward Eden and Dee Goertz. Toronto: University of Toronto Press, 2003. 39–60.

Gilbert, Sandra, and Susan Gubar. *The Madwoman in the Attic: The Woman Writer and the Nineteenth-Century Literary Imagination*. New Haven: Yale University Press, 1979.

Gilmore, Leigh. *Autobiographics: A Feminist Theory of Women's Self-Representation*. Ithaca: Cornell University Press, 1994.

– "The Mark of Autobiography: Postmodernism, Autobiography, and Genre." In *Autobiography and Postmodernism*. Ed. Kathleen Ashley, Leigh Gilmore, and Gerald Peters. Amherst: University of Massachusetts Press, 1994. 3–18.

Girard, René. *The Girard Reader*. 1996. Edited by James G. Williams. New York: Crossroad, 2001.

Grescoe, Paul. "Eulogy for a Poet." *Canadian Magazine*, 5 June 1976, 13, 16–19.

Groening, Laura. "Still in the Kitchen: The Art of Carol Shields." *Canadian Forum* 69 (Jan./Feb. 1991): 14–17.

Gzowski, Peter. ""Pat Lowther: Woman, Mother, Artist." Producer Alan Safarik. "Gzowski on FM." *CBC Radio*, 2 Nov. 1975, 2.

Hall, Susan Grove. "The Duality of the Artist/Crafter in Carol Shields's Novels." *Kentucky Philological Review* 12 (1997): 42–7.

Hammill, Faye. "Carol Shields's 'Native Genre' and the Figure of the Canadian Author." *Journal of Commonwealth Literature* 31.2 (1996): 87–99. http://dx.doi.org/10.1177/002198949603100208.

– "Influential Circles: Carol Shields and the Canadian Literary Canon." In *Literary Culture and Female Authorship in Canada 1760–2000*. Amsterdam: Rodopi, 2003. 115–33.

– "*The Republic of Love* and Popular Romance." In *Carol Shields, Narrative Hunger, and the Possibilities of Fiction*. Ed. Edward Eden and Dee Goertz. Toronto: University of Toronto Press, 2003. 61–83.

Hansson, Heidi. "Biography Matters: Carol Shields, *Mary Swann*, A.S. Byatt, *Possession*, Deborah Crombie, *Dreaming of the Bones*." *Orbis Litterarum: International Review of Literary Studies* 58.5 (2003): 353–70. http://dx.doi.org/10.1034/j.1600-0730.2003.00779.x.

Hawthorn, Jeremy. *A Glossary of Contemporary Literary Theory*. 4th ed. New York: Oxford University Press, 2000.

Hennessy, Rosemary. *Materialist Feminism and the Politics of Discourse*. New York: Routledge, 1993.

Herbert, George. "Love (III)." In *The Literature of Renaissance England*. Ed. John Hollander and Frank Kermode. New York: Oxford University Press, 1973. 678.

Hobbs, Catherine. "Archives as Traces of Life Process and Engagement: The Late Years of the Carol Shields Fonds." In *The Worlds of Carol Shields*. Ed. David Staines. Ottawa: University of Ottawa Press, 2014. 277–92.

Hollenberg, Donna Krolik, and Carol Shields. "An Interview with Carol Shields." *Contemporary Literature* 39.3 (1998): 339–55. http://dx.doi.org/10.2307/1208862.

Howells, Coral Ann. *Contemporary Canadian Women's Fiction: Refiguring Identities*. New York: Palgrave Macmillan, 2003. http://dx.doi.org/10.1057/9781403973542.

Hutcheon, Linda. *The Canadian Postmodern: A Study of Contemporary English-Canadian Fiction*. Toronto: Oxford University Press, 1988.

– "Postmodernism." In *Encyclopedia of Contemporary Literary Theory: Approaches, Scholars, Terms*. Ed. Irene R. Makaryk. Toronto: University of Toronto Press, 1993. 612–13.

– "The Power of Postmodern Irony." In *Genre, Trope, Gender: Critical Essays*. Ed. Northrop Frye, Linda Hutcheon, and Shirley Neuman. Ottawa: Carleton University Press, 1992. 35–49.

Hutcheon, Linda, Northrop Frye, and Shirley Neuman, eds. *Genre, Trope, Gender: Critical Essays*. Ottawa: Carleton University Press, 1992.

Irvine, Lorna. "A Knowable Country: Embodied Omniscience in Carol Shields's *The Republic of Love* and *Larry's Party*." In *Carol Shields and the Extra-Ordinary*. Ed. Marta Dvorak and Manina Jones. Montreal: McGill-Queen's University Press, 2007. 139–56.

Jameson, Fredric. *The Political Unconscious: Narrative as a Socially Symbolic Act*. Ithaca: Cornell University Press, 1981.

– "Postmodernism and Consumer Society." In *The Anti-Aesthetic: Essays on Postmodern Culture*. Ed. Hal Foster. Port Townsend: Bay Press, 1983. 111–25.

Johnson, Brian. "Necessary Illusions: Foucault's Author Function in Carol Shields's *Swann*." In *Carol Shields: The Arts of a Writing Life*. Ed. Neil K. Besner. Winnipeg: Prairie Fire Press, 2003. 209–28.

Johnson, Randal. "*Editor's Introduction*: Pierre Bourdieu on Art, Literature and Culture." In *The Field of Cultural Production*. Edited by Randal Johnson. New York: Columbia University Press, 1993. 1–25.

Kadar, Marlene. "The Discourse of Ordinariness and 'Multicultural History.'" *Essays on Canadian Writing* 60 (1996): 119–38.

Kadar, Marlene, ed. *Essays on Life Writing: From Genre to Critical Practice*. Toronto: University of Toronto Press, 1992.

Kavka, Misha. "Introduction." In *Feminist Consequences: Theory for the New Century*. Ed. Elisabeth Bronfen and Misha Kavka. New York: Columbia University Press, 2001. ix–xxvi.

Lane, Patrick. "Pat Lowther, c. 1973." *Geist* 17 (1975): 30.

Lanser, Susan Sniader. *Fictions of Authority: Women Writers and Narrative Voice*. Ithaca: Cornell University Press, 1992.

Lejeune, Philippe. "The Autobiographical Pact." In *On Autobiography*. Edited by Paul John Eakin. Translated by Katherine Leary. Minneapolis: University of Minnesota Press, 1989. 3–30.

– "The Autobiographical Pact (bis)." In *On Autobiography*. Edited by Paul John Eakin. Translated by Katherine Leary. Minneapolis: University of Minnesota Press, 1989. 119–37.

Lessing, Doris. *The Golden Notebook*. 1962. Toronto: Grafton Books, 1986.

Lowther, Pat. *The Age of the Bird*. Vancouver: Blackfish Press, 1972.

– *The Collected Works of Pat Lowther*. Ed. Christine Wiesenthal. Edmonton: NeWest Press, 2010.

– *This Difficult Flowering*. Vancouver: Very Stone House, 1968.

– *Final Instructions*. Vancouver: West Coast Review / Orca Sound, 1980.

– *Milk Stone*. Ottawa: Borealis Press, 1974.

– *A Stone Diary*. Toronto: Oxford University Press, 1977.

– *Time Capsule: New and Selected Poems*. Victoria: Polestar Books, 1996.

MacDonald, Bruce F. "Quiet Manifesto: Carol Shields's *Small Ceremonies*." *International Fiction Review* 3.9 (1976): 147–50.

Maharaj, Robyn. "'The Arc of a Whole Life': A Telephone Interview with Carol Shields from Her Home in Victoria, BC, May 4, 2002." *Prairie Fire* 23.4 (2002/2003): 8–11.

Marlatt, Daphne. "Self-Representation and Fictionalysis." In *Collaboration in the Feminine: Writings on Women and Culture from Tessera*. Ed. Barbara Godard. Toronto: Second Story Press, 1994. 202–6.

– "Writing Our Way through the Labyrinth." In *Collaboration in the Feminine: Writings on Women and Culture from Tessera*. Ed. Barbara Godard. Toronto: Second Story Press, 1994. 44–6.

Martin, Wallace. *Recent Theories of Narrative*. Ithaca: Cornell University Press, 1986.

Mayne, Seymour. "For Pat Lowther (1935–1975)." In *The Impossible Promised Land: Poems New and Selected*. Oakville: Mosaic Press, 1981. 118.

McHale, Brian. *Postmodernist Fiction*. New York: Methuen, 1987. http://dx.doi.org/10.4324/9780203393321.

McMullen, Lorraine. "Carol Shields and the University of Ottawa: Some Reminiscences." In *Carol Shields: The Arts of a Writing Life*. Ed. Neil K. Besner. Winnipeg: Prairie Fire Press, 2003. 39–46.

Moi, Toril. "Appropriating Bourdieu: Feminist Theory and Pierre Bourdieu's Sociology of Culture." *New Literary History* 22.4 (1991): 1017–49. http://dx.doi.org/10.2307/469077.

Moses, Daniel David. "Our Lady of the Glacier." In *First Person Plural*. Ed. Judith Fitzgerald. Windsor: Black Moss Press, 1988. 46–7.

Muecke, Stephen. "The Fall: Fictocritical Writing." *Parallax* 8.4 (2002): 108–12. http://dx.doi.org/10.1080/1353464022000028000.

Nettelbeck, Amanda. "Notes toward an Introduction." In *The Space Between: Australian Women Writing Fictocriticism*. Ed. Heather Kerr and Amanda Nettelbeck. Melbourne: University of Western Australia Press, 1998. 1–17.

Neuman, Shirley. "Introduction: Reading Canadian Autobiography." *Essays on Canadian Writing* 60 (1996): 1–13.

Niederhoff, Burkhard. "How to Do Things with History: Researching Lives in Carol Shields's *Swann* and Margaret Atwood's *Alias Grace*." *Journal of Commonwealth Literature* 35.2 (2000): 71–85.

Nodelman, Perry. "Living in the Republic of Love: Carol Shields's Winnipeg." In *Carol Shields: The Arts of a Writing Life*. Ed. Neil K. Besner. Winnipeg: Prairie Fire Press, 2003. 105–24.

Ondaatje, Michael. *Running in the Family*. Toronto: McClelland and Stewart, 1982.

Page, Malcolm. "*Small Ceremonies* and the Art of the Novel." *Journal of Canadian Fiction* 28–29 (1980): 172–8.

Prince, Gerald. *A Dictionary of Narratology*. Lincoln: University of Nebraska Press, 1987.

Proust, Marcel. *A la recherche du temps perdu*. Paris: Gallimard, 1987.

Ramon, Alex. *Liminal Spaces: The Double Art of Carol Shields*. Newcastle-upon-Tyne: Cambridge Scholars, 2008.

Randolph, Jeanne. "Out of Psychoanalysis: A Ficto-Criticism Monologue." In *Canadian Cultural Poesis: Essays on Canadian Culture*. Ed. Garry Sherbert, Anne Gérin, and Sheila Petty. Waterloo: Wilfrid Laurier University Press, 2006. 231–47.

Rapaport, Herman. "The New Personalism." *Biography* 21.1 (1998): 36–49. http://dx.doi.org/10.1353/bio.2010.0045.

Reineke, Martha. "The Mother in Mimesis: Kristeva and Girard on Violence and the Sacred." In *Body/Text in Julia Kristeva: Religion, Women, and Psychoanalysis*. Ed. David R. Crownfield. Albany: State University of New York Press, 1992. 67–85.

Riegel, Christian. "Carol Shields (2 June 1935 – 16 July 2003)." In *Dictionary of Literary Biography*, vol. 334, *Twenty-First-Century Canadian Writers*. Ed. Christian Riegel. Detroit: Thomson Gale, 2007. 206–17.

Rimmon-Kenan, Shlomith. *Narrative Fiction: Contemporary Poetics*. 1983. 2nd ed. London: Routledge, 2002.

Roberts, Gillian. *Prizing Literature: The Celebration and Circulation of National Culture*. Toronto: University of Toronto Press, 2011.

Rooke, Constance. "Shields, Carol (b. 1935)." In *The Oxford Companion to Canadian Literature*. Ed. William Toye. Toronto: Oxford University Press, 1983. 751–2; *The Oxford Companion to Canadian Literature*. 2nd ed. Ed. Eugene Benson and William Toye. Don Mills: Oxford University Press, 1997. 1057.

Roy, Wendy. "Autobiography as Critical Practice in *The Stone Diaries*." In *Carol Shields, Narrative Hunger, and the Possibilities of Fiction*. Ed. Edward Eden and Dee Goertz. Toronto: University of Toronto Press, 2003. 113–46.

– "*Unless* the World Changes: Carol Shields on Women's Silencing in Contemporary Culture." In *Carol Shields: The Arts of a Writing Life*. Ed. Neil K. Besner. Winnipeg: Prairie Fire Press, 2003. 125–32.

Schnitzer, Deborah. "Tricks and Artful Photographs and Letters in Carol Shields's *The Stone Diaries* and Anita Brookner's *Hotel du Lac*." In *Carol Shields: The Arts of a Writing Life*. Ed. Neil Besner. Winnipeg: Prairie Fire Press, 2003. 145–59.

Sherbert, Garry H. "Introduction: A Poetics of Canadian Culture." In *Canadian Cultural Poesis: Essays on Canadian Culture*. Ed. Garry Sherbert, Anne Gérin, and Sheila Petty. Waterloo: Wilfrid Laurier University Press, 2006. 1–22.

Shields, Carol. "Afterword." In *Life in the Clearings versus the Bush*, by Susanna Moodie. Toronto: McClelland and Stewart, 1989. 335–40.

– "Arriving Late: Starting Over." In *How Stories Mean*. Ed. John Metcalf and J.R. Struthers. Erin, Ont.: Porcupine's Quill, 1993. 244–51.

– *The Box Garden*. 1977. Toronto: Vintage, 1990.

– "The Ineffable Mystery of Personality." *Globe and Mail*, 17 Sept. 1988, F13.

– *Jane Austen: A Life*. New York: Viking, 2001.

– "Jane Austen Images of the Body: No Fingers, No Toes." *Persuasions: Journal of the Jane Austen Society of North America* 13 (1991): 132–7.

– *Larry's Party*. Toronto: Vintage, 1997.

– "Leaving the Brick House Behind: Margaret Laurence and the Loop of Memory." *Recherches anglaises et nord-americaines* 24 (1991): 75–7.

– "'My Craft and Sullen Art': The Writers Speak." With Dorothy Livesay, Miriam Waddington, Beth Harvor, Audrey Thomas, Gwen Pharis Ringwood. *Atlantis: A Women's Studies Journal* 4.1 (1978): 143–52.

– "Narrative Hunger and the Overflowing Cupboard."In *Carol Shields, Narrative Hunger, and the Possibilities of Fiction*. Ed. Edward Eden and Dee Goertz. Toronto: University of Toronto Press, 2003. 19–36.

– *The Republic of Love*. 1992. Toronto: Vintage, 1994.

– Rev. of *Ruby: An Ordinary Woman*. *Boston Globe*, 30 April 1995, B15, B18.

– *Small Ceremonies*. 1976. Toronto: Vintage, 1995.

– *The Stone Diaries*. Toronto: Random House, 1993.

– *Susanna Moodie: Voice and Vision*. 1972. Ottawa: Borealis, 1977.

– *Swann*. 1987. Toronto: Random House, 1995.

– "'Thinking Back through Our Mothers': Tradition in Canadian Women's Writing." In *Re(Dis)covering Our Foremothers: Nineteenth-Century Canadian Women Writers*. Ed. Lorraine McMullen. Ottawa: University of Ottawa Press, 1990. 5–21.

– "Three Canadian Women: Fiction or Autobiography?" *Atlantis: A Women's Studies Journal* 4.1 (1978): 49–54.

– *Unless*. Toronto: Random House, 2002.

– *Various Miracles*. Toronto: Vintage, 1985.

Shields, Carol, and Blanche Howard. 1991. *A Celibate Season*. Toronto: Vintage, 1998.

"Shields, Carol (b. 1935)." In *The Concise Oxford Companion to Canadian Literature*. Ed. William Toye. Don Mills: Oxford University Press, 2001. 442–4.

"Shields, Carol, 1935." In *Contemporary Canadian Authors*. Ed. Robert Lang. Toronto: Gale Canada, 1996. 418–19.

Sims Brandon, Lisa. "Revisiting Sleepy Hollow: An Analysis of Edna in *The Awakening* and Daisy in *The Stone Diaries*." *Publications of the Mississippi Philological Association* (1996): 1–5.

Smith, Paul. *Discerning the Subject*. Minneapolis: University of Minnesota Press, 1988.

Smith, Sidonie. *A Poetics of Women's Autobiography: Marginality and the Fictions of Self-Representation*. Bloomington: Indiana University Press, 1987.

Smith, Sidonie, and Julia Watson. *Reading Autobiography: A Guide for Interpreting Life Narratives*. Minneapolis: University of Minnesota Press, 2001.

Spettigue, D.O. "Grove, Frederick Philip (1879–1948)." In *The Oxford Companion to Canadian Literature*. Ed. William Toye. Toronto: Oxford University Press, 1983. 324–7.

Staels, Hilde. "Verbalisation of Loss in Carol Shields' *The Stone Diaries* and *Unless*." *Zeitschrift für Kanada-Studien* 24.2 (2004): 118–31.

Staines, David, ed. *The Worlds of Carol Shields*. Ottawa: University of Ottawa Press, 2014.

Steenman-Marcusse, Conny. "Carol Shields' *Small Ceremonies*: Susanna Moodie and Her Biographer Judith Gill." In *Re-writing Pioneer Women in Anglo-Canadian Literature*. Amsterdam: Rodopi, 2001. 93–125.

Steffler, Margaret. "A Human Conversation about Goodness: Carol Shields's *Unless*." *Studies in Canadian Literature* 34.2 (2009): 223–44.

Stelzig, Eugene L. "Poetry and/or Truth: An Essay on the Confessional Imagination." *University of Toronto Quarterly* 54.4 (1984): 17–37. http://dx.doi.org/10.3138/utq.54.1.17.

Stovel, Nora Foster. "'Because She's a Woman': Myth and Metafiction in Carol Shields's *Unless*." *English Studies in Canada* 32.4 (2006): 51–73. http://dx.doi.org/10.1353/esc.0.0014.

Sugars, Cynthia. "Bio-Critical Afterlives: Sarah Binks, Pat Lowther, and the Satirical Gothic Turn in Carol Shields's *Swann*." In *The Worlds of Carol Shields*. Ed. David Staines. Ottawa: University of Ottawa Press, 2014. 81–92.

Sweeney, Susan Elizabeth. "Formal Strategies in a Female Narrative Tradition: The Case of *Swann: A Mystery*." In *Anxious Power: Reading, Writing, and Ambivalence in Narrative by Women*. Ed. Carol J. Singley and Susan Elizabeth Sweeney. Albany: State University of New York Press, 1993. 19–32.

"The 90s: A Look Back at Some of the Decade's Most Notable Books." *Quill & Quire* 66.1 (2000): 41.

Thomas, Clara. "Carol Shields: *The Republic of Love* and *The Stone Diaries*. 'Swerves of Destiny' and 'Rings of Light.'" In *"Union in Partition": Essays in Honour of Jeanne Delbaere*. Ed. Gilbert Debusscher and Marc Maufort. Liège: L-3 Liège Language and Literature, 1997. 153–60.

– "Reassembling Fragments: Susanna Moodie, Carol Shields, and Mary Swann." In *Inside the Poem: Essays and Poems in Honour of Donald Stephens*. Ed. W.H. New. Toronto: Oxford University Press, 1992. 196–204.

– "'A Slight Parodic Edge': Swann: A Mystery." *Room of One's Own: A Feminist Journal of Literature and Criticism* 13.1–2 (1989): 109–22.

Thomas, Hilda L. "Pat Lowther, July 29, 1935–September 24, 1975." In *Dictionary of Literary Biography*, vol. 53, *Canadian Writers Since 1960, First Series*. Ed. W.H. New. Detroit: Thomson Gale, 1986. 276–8.

Thomas, Joan. "'The Golden Book': An Interview with Carol Shields." *Prairie Fire Press* 14.4 (1993–94): 56–62.

Thompson, Kent. "Reticence in Carol Shields." *Room of One's Own: A Feminist Journal of Literature and Criticism* 13.1–2 (1989): 69–76.

Tolstoy, Leo. *The Death of Ivan Ilyich*. 1981. Translated by Lynn Solotaroff. New York: Bantam Books, 1990.

Tuhkunen, Taïna. "Carol Shields's *The Republic of Love*, or How to Ravish a Genre." In *Carol Shields and the Extra-Ordinary*. Ed. Marta Dvorak and Manina Jones. Montreal: McGill-Queen's University Press, 2007. 97–114.

Van Herk, Aritha. *In Visible Ink: Crypto-frictions*. Edmonton: NeWest Press, 1991.

Van Herk, Aritha, and Conny Steenman-Marcusse, eds. *Carol Shields: Evocation and Echo*. Groningen: Barkhuis, 2009.

Vauthier, Simone. "On Carol Shields's 'Mrs Turner Cutting the Grass.'" *Commonwealth Essays and Studies* 11.2 (1989): 63–74.

– "Ruptures in Carol Shields's *The Stone Diaries*." *Anglophonia: French Journal of English Studies* 1 (1997): 177–92.

– "'They Say Miracles Are Past' but They Are Wrong." In *Carol Shields: The Arts of a Writing Life*. Ed. Neil K. Besner. Winnipeg: Prairie Fire Press, 2003. 183–208.

Veeser, H. Aram. "Introduction: The Case for Confessional Criticism." In *Confessions of the Critics: North American Critics' Autobiographical Moves*. New York: Routledge, 1996. ix–xxvii.

Wachtel, Eleanor. "Interview with Carol Shields." *Room of One's Own: A Feminist Journal of Literature and Criticism* 13.1–2 (1989): 5–45.

– "Introduction." *Room of One's Own: A Feminist Journal of Literature and Criticism* 13.1–2 (1989): 2–4.

– *Random Illuminations: Conversations with Carol Shields*. Fredericton: Goose Lane Editions, 2007.

Watt, Ian P. *The Rise of the Novel: Studies in Defoe, Richardson and Fielding*.
  1957. Berkeley: University of California Press, 1971.
Wiesenthal, Christine. *The Half-Lives of Pat Lowther*. Toronto: University of
  Toronto Press, 2005.
Williams, David. "Making Stories, Making Selves: 'Alternate Versions' in
  The Stone Diaries." *Canadian Literature* 186 (2005): 10–28.
– "Re-imagining a Stone Angel: The Absent Autobiographer of *The Stone
  Diaries*." In *O Canada: Essays on Canadian Literature and Culture*. Ed. Jørn
  Carlsen and Tim Caudrey. Aarhus, Denmark: Aarhus University Press,
  1995. 126–41.
Woodcock, George. "The Muse of Manawaka." *100 Great Canadians*.
  Edmonton: Hurtig, 1980. 157–9.
Woolf, Virginia. *A Room of One's Own*. 1929. London: Grafton, 1977.
York, Lorraine. *Literary Celebrity in Canada*. Toronto: University of Toronto
  Press, 2007.
– "Shields, Carol." In *Encyclopedia of Literature in Canada*. Ed. W.H. New.
  Toronto: University of Toronto Press, 2002. 1037–8.

Index

Lightning Source UK Ltd.
Milton Keynes UK
UKOW01f1700070416

271764UK00003B/277/P